THE ROAR OF JUSTICE

HEARING GOD'S RELENTLESS CALL IN THE BOOK OF AMOS

VANESSA K. HAWKINS

An imprint of InterVarsity Press
Downers Grove, Illinois

InterVarsity Press
P.O. Box 1400, Downers Grove, IL 60515-1426
ivpress.com
email@ivpress.com

InterVarsity Press® is the publishing division of InterVarsity Christian Fellowship/USA®. For more information, visit intervarsity.org.

Cover design: Gearbox with Faceout Studio
Interior design: Jeanna Wiggins
Cover images: © LiuSol / iStock via Getty Images, © Queso / iStock via Getty Images

ISBN 978-1-5140-1158-4 (print) | ISBN 978-1-5140-1159-1 (digital)

Printed in the United States of America ♾

Library of Congress Cataloging-in-Publication Data
Names: Hawkins, Vanessa K., 1973- author
Title: The roar of justice : hearing God's relentless call in the book of Amos : an 8-week Bible study with video access / Vanessa K. Hawkins.
Description: Downers Grove, IL : IVP , [2026] | Series: IVP Bible study experience | Includes bibliographical references.
Identifiers: LCCN 2025041886 (print) | LCCN 2025041887 (ebook) | ISBN 9781514011584 paperback | ISBN 9781514011591 ebook
Subjects: LCSH: Bible. Amos–Criticism, interpretation, etc. | Justice–Biblical teaching | Bible–Study and teaching
Classification: LCC BS1585.6.J8 H39 2026 (print) | LCC BS1585.6.J8 (ebook)
LC record available at https://lccn.loc.gov/2025041886
LC ebook record available at https://lccn.loc.gov/2025041887

31 30 29 28 27 26 | 8 7 6 5 4 3 2 1

"In *The Roar of Justice*, Vanessa K. Hawkins invites us to listen closely to God's Word and see that God's heart for justice is not only a theme in Amos but a resounding thread woven throughout all of Scripture. She shows that God's justice is not just a topic for discussion—it is part of who he is and how he calls us to live. This powerful study will help you hear God's voice more clearly and experience his heart for the flourishing of all people."

Courtney Doctor, director of women's initiatives at The Gospel Coalition and author of *From Garden to Glory*

"In his book *The Prophets*, Abraham J. Heschel wrote, 'Justice is a divine concern.' However, many disciples of Jesus Christ are befuddled by what justice means and how to do justice. Fortunately, my former seminary and Sunday school student Vanessa K. Hawkins has generously gifted us a thoughtfully designed and biblically grounded interactive study toward making God's concern for doing justice our concern as well. Praise God for Hawkins and her good and timely work, *The Roar of Justice*!"

Luke Brad Bobo, cofounder of Pursuing the Greater Good LLC

"Many Christians today would have a hard time just naming a minor prophet in the Bible, much less knowing and applying Amos as God's living word for us today. In our highly polarized world, it is no wonder that Christians are often unsure of what to believe about crucial biblical issues like justice, poverty, idolatry, repentance, and mercy. These are the exact themes that the minor prophets confronted God's people about when they began to lose their way. Vanessa K. Hawkins has done us all an enormous service by creating a study guide for one of the most important, yet least studied, minor prophets."

Abraham Cho, vice president for thought leadership at Redeemer City to City and author of *Joyful Resistance: A Serious Call for Happy Non-Conformists*

"Justice has become a hot-button issue in our churches. Merely reading the Word as it occurs in a text of Scripture can send the hypervigilant to their well-run ruts on the cultural left or right. My friend Vanessa Hawkins is a nonanxious leader, and it comes out in this study. To study the Bible on justice, she says, requires looking into the heart of God. That will calm, convict, and commission us to participate in the Father's just mission, which cost him his only begotten Son."

George Robertson, senior pastor of Second Presbyterian Memphis and author of *Soul Anatomy*

CONTENTS

INTRODUCTION		1
WEEK 1	THE LION ROARS	7
WEEK 2	ISRAEL HEARS THE ROAR	29
WEEK 3	YOU ONLY HAVE I KNOWN	45
WEEK 4	RETURN TO THE LORD	61
WEEK 5	LET JUSTICE ROLL DOWN	81
WEEK 6	CONFRONTING THE IDOL OF COMFORT	101
WEEK 7	COMPASSION: THE COMPANION TO JUSTICE	123
WEEK 8	RESTORING PEOPLE AND REBUILDING PLACES	147
BENEDICTION		163
NOTES		165
RESOURCES		167
FIGURE CREDITS		169

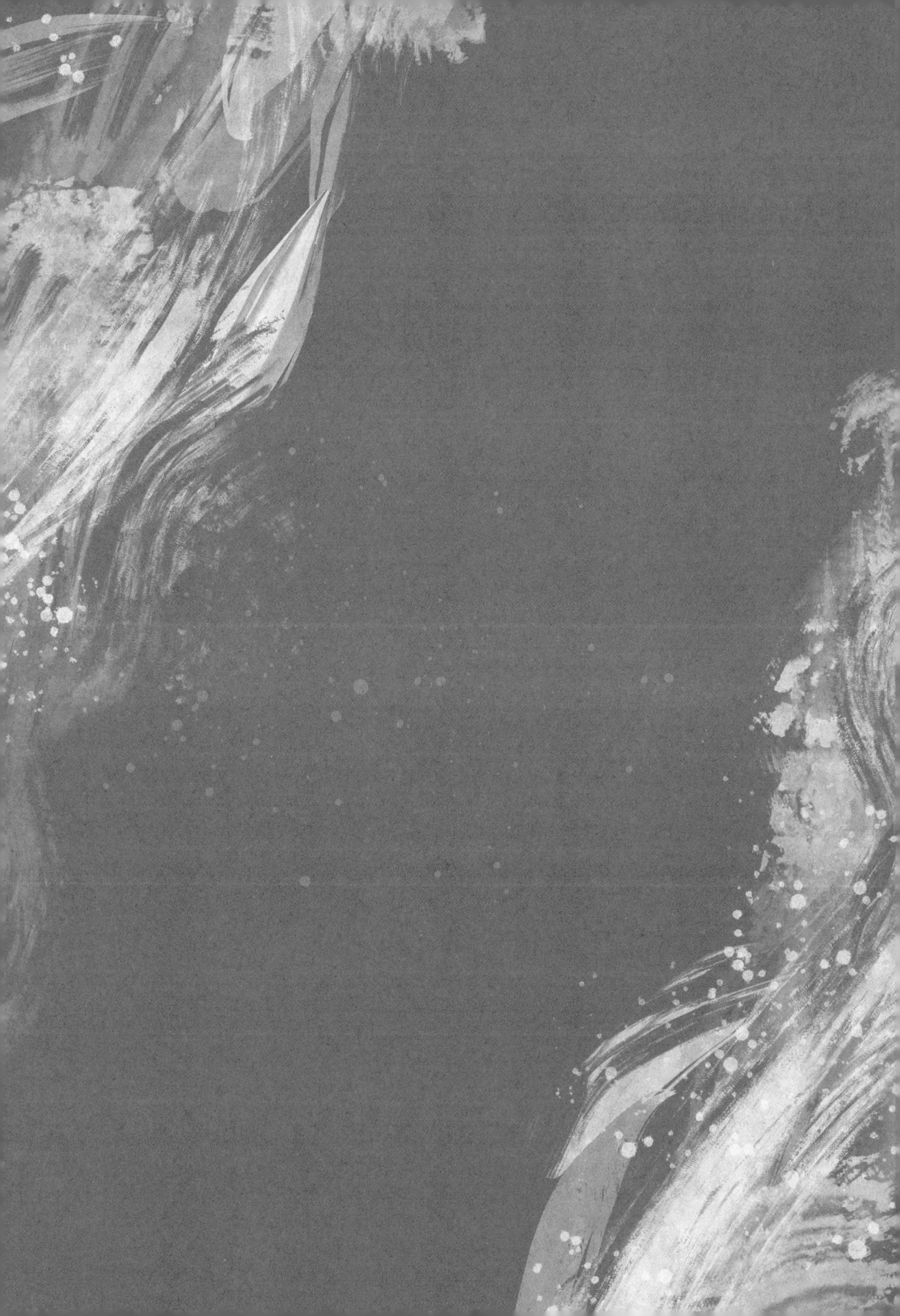

INTRODUCTION

INJUSTICE. It's that deep churning of the soul, the kind that presses tightly between your ribs before finally spilling out in exasperation—"This is not right!" The cry of injustice wells up from deep within until it can no longer hold its peace. It's the sentiment of anyone being wronged or defending the cause of another. The sense of injustice is innate in the toddler who declares, "That's not fair" or the brave kid who stands up to the playground bully. It's at the core of every march, every protest—from the Boston Tea Party to the Civil Rights Movement. Whether the wrongs represent years of inequity or a cataclysmic event putting the spotlight on a disadvantaged people group, each situation raises the questions: What is justice? What is the standard for what is good and right? And what is our role in making right what is wrong?

To think rightly about justice we must necessarily consider the heart of the Righteous Judge as revealed through the pages of Scripture. It is often the case that we turn to a few verses that explicitly state our need to pursue justice, i.e., "To act justly and to love mercy and to walk humbly with your God" (Micah 6:8), or "But let justice roll on like a river, righteousness like a never-failing stream" (Amos 5:24). While these passages certainly reflect the Father's heart for justice, they are mere tributaries that flow out of a mighty undercurrent of justice coursing through the entirety of Scripture. In isolation, these passages trickle whispers of disconnected thoughts, but when properly understood, they are one continuous, mighty stream flowing from the unchanging character of God.

The book of Amos is an outflow of this stream, expressing the universal justice of God. As this unlikely shepherd prophet expresses warnings to Israel and surrounding nations, we hear the heart of God expressed not in a whisper but in a roar—for all people and all times. If we listen closely, we hear what God values and what he detests. We hear his desire for the flourishing of humanity and evidence of his righteous rule over all nations. Amos ultimately requires that we look to the day when the Father's justice is satisfied through the death and resurrection of his Son and to the day when he comes again to make all things new. He challenges us to think sober-mindedly as the roar of God's justice echoes to all who are willing to hear. It is my hope that within the pages of this study, you will hear the heart of God and be strengthened to participate in the restorative work he's doing in your part of the world.

WHAT THIS STUDY IS NOT

The polarizing tenor of our cultural moment complicates just about any discussion on justice. Just mention the word *justice*, and questions and suspicions immediately surface concerning motive and exactly what is meant when you say "justice." Are you talking about social justice? Are you subscribing to some kind of "woke" ideology or a drift toward liberalism? Some will hear the word *justice* and immediately wonder if this is talking about Critical Race Theory. I want to assure you that this study is about none of the above.

This study was born out of a desire to hear God's heart about justice in a climate where injustices in the broader culture are frequent and polarizing. Resulting fear, injury, and frustration produce many loud voices, but the loudest voice isn't always the voice of truth. To really understand justice, it is necessary that we understand the heart of God, who is the Righteous Judge. If justice is something that is optional for God, then it should absolutely be optional for us. But if it is a primary value and an outflow of God's very heart, then it becomes essential that we understand how to participate in his setting things right in his world, by being agents of restoration, a restorative presence in our spheres of influence. It is necessary for us to understand how God thinks about justice.

HOW TO GET THE MOST FROM THIS STUDY

While the book of Amos is an often-neglected part of Scripture, all of Scripture is the breathed out, living Word of God (2 Timothy 3:16). And anything that God breathes out, we can be sure it is well worth our breathing in! The prophet Isaiah reminds us that "The Sovereign Lord has given me a well-instructed tongue, to know the word that sustains the weary. He wakens me morning by morning, wakens my ear to listen like one being instructed" (Isaiah 50:4). The Author of Scripture himself is willing to meet with us to lead us and instruct us through the pages of his Holy Word.

PRAYER

The opening prayer for each day is a way of pausing and remembering truth as we seek understanding from the very Word of God. Pausing to pray also helps us resist the temptation to rely merely on our intellect to understand words that are breathed out by the Spirit of the living God. Regular rhythms of talking to the Author about his words will aid us in rightly subordinating ourselves under Scripture's authority and humbly seeking the God of the Scriptures for understanding.

READ

Before you begin this book, it would be helpful to read through or listen to the entire book of Amos to gain some familiarity with its content and flow. Reading and re-reading your study passage each day will deepen your understanding. You might be surprised at how prayerful re-reading will cause you to see something new and gain greater insight.

GROUP SESSION

Each week I will provide a brief introduction, with historical and cultural context for the passage we will be studying. I want to emphasize that this will be simply an introduction, an overview that invites you into the passage, hopefully piquing your curiosity and helping you grow as a Bible student who asks good questions of the text.

The group sessions are designed to help you think through major themes of the lesson for the week. A ten- to fifteen-minute video teaching and group discussion questions will prompt you to articulate how you think about these themes of the study. The discussion questions are designed to capture your heart attitude as you approach the week's study. When coupled with the "respond" section on day five of the study, these discussion questions will serve as a practical and powerful demonstration of how you are being informed and transformed by the Scriptures.

FIVE-DAY INDIVIDUAL STUDY

Like the veritable feast the Word of God is, it is not meant to be gulped down in one sitting but savored and enjoyed over many courses. The study is arranged in the following five-day format for individual study and reflection:

Day 1—What does the text say? Here we will observe the text, noting repetitions, contrasts, explanations, and questions. We'll pay attention to the who, what, where, and when of the text, its verbs, pronouns, modifiers, and anything else we might have questions about.

Days 2 and 3—What does the text mean? On days two and three we will begin to make meaning of what we observed by defining words, phrases, and concepts. Here is a good place to chart the flow of the author's thought or argument and check our interpretation against secondary sources such as good study Bible notes or a commentary.

Defining our terms. These sections will give us a common vocabulary by which to discuss the nuances of justice throughout the book of Amos.

On reading the prophets well. Each week you will be given instruction on "Reading the Prophets Well" that will help you build a toolkit, an interpretive grid of sorts, for making meaning out of the book of Amos and other prophetical books—both major and minor.

Day 4—What does the rest of Scripture say? In this section of study, we will compare our text with similar themes found in other places in Scripture. This will aid our interpretation and help us see Scripture as one continuous story and not just isolated passages.

Day 5—Reflections: practicing justice. Day five is where the theology of justice meets the practice of justice. For many, justice is an intimidating notion, as the injustices we are aware of are far more than what we can reasonably address. The practicing justice section will guide us in developing an awareness of injustices in our current spheres and in considering how we can be a restorative presence in those spaces.

MY PRAYER FOR YOU

Through this study, may you encounter the God of the Scriptures, know him more fully, and worship him deeply. May the outflow of this love for him be radical love for your neighbor, evidenced in new awareness of the suffering of others and fresh conviction to be a restorative presence wherever you are.

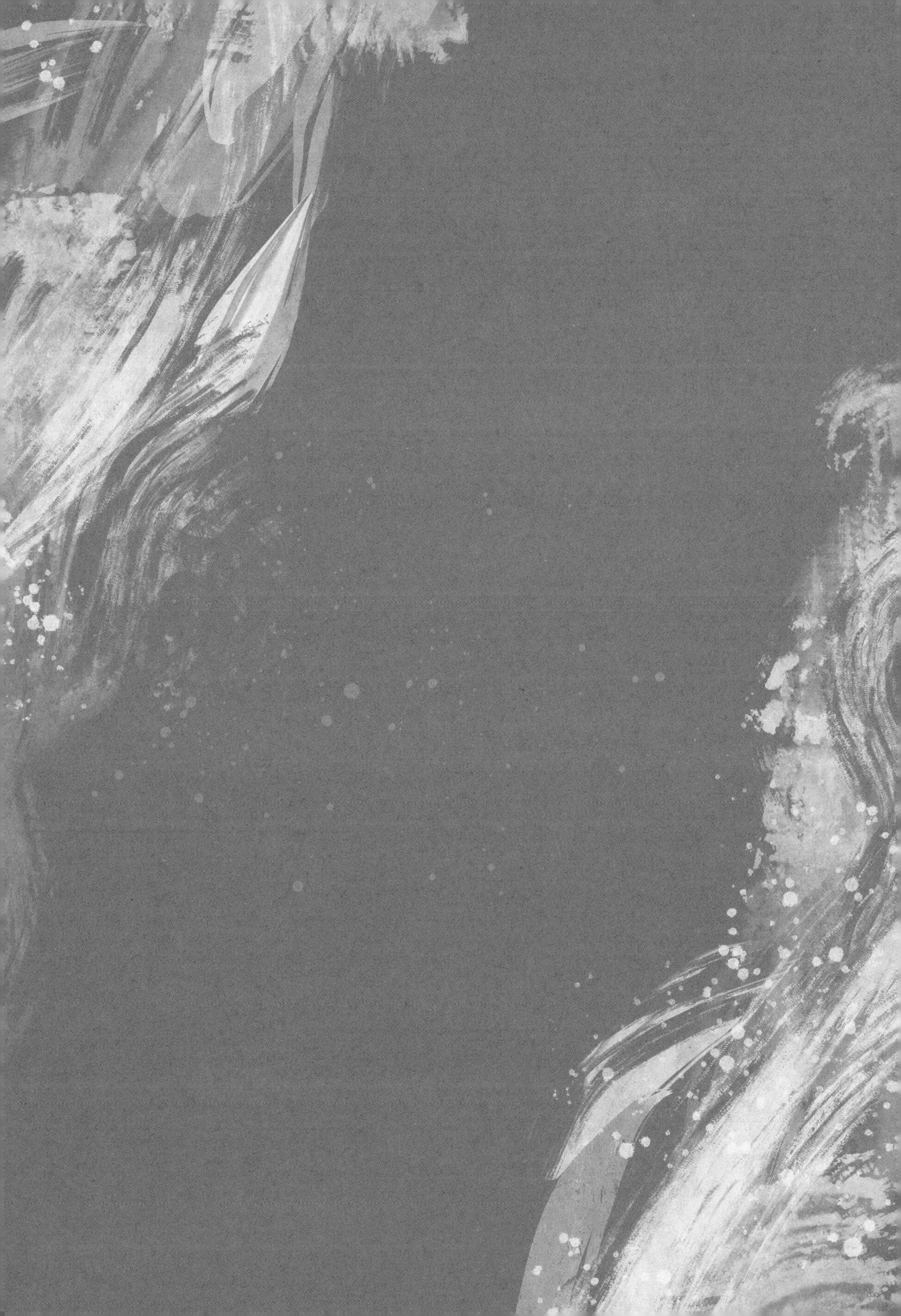

WEEK 1
THE LION ROARS

So God created mankind in his own image, in the image of God
he created them; male and female he created them.

GENESIS 1:27

GROUP SESSION INTRODUCTION

The introductory verse of the book of Amos is jam-packed with rich information that sets us in the sandy soils of the ancient Near East. In the very next verse, we experience the vivid imagery of a lion roaring and all of creation responding.

> The words of Amos, one of the shepherds of Tekoa—the vision he saw concerning Israel two years before the earthquake, when Uzziah was king of Judah and Jeroboam son of Jehoash was king of Israel.
>
> He said:
>
> "The Lord roars from Zion
> and thunders from Jerusalem;
> the pastures of the shepherds dry up,
> and the top of Carmel withers." (Amos 1:1-2)

OPENING PRAYER

Lord, open our eyes and show us wonderful things in this portion of Scripture. More than informed, help us to be transformed by the renewing of our minds by the power of your Spirit, in Jesus' name, amen. (from Psalm 119:18 and Romans 12:2)

SCRIPTURE

Read aloud Amos 1:1–2:5.

VIDEO

Watch this week's video.

GROUP DISCUSSION

1. What fears do you have about reading the prophets? Have you studied a prophetic book before, either major or minor? Discuss any experience you have had with the prophets as a genre of Scripture.
2. A prophet's role brought a great compulsion to speak God's words—what difficulties might they have faced in calling people to repentance?
3. In 2 Timothy 3:16, we are reminded that all Scripture is God-breathed and useful for training in righteousness. How are you hoping to be instructed through the prophet Amos?
4. Of the common obstacles to reading the book of Amos, which challenge resonates most with you: the perception of God as wrathful, the difficulty of the text, the relevance to today, or the co-opting of the word *justice*?
5. The prophet Amos depicts the Lord as a lion roaring in response to injustice—to crimes against those made in his image—not only in Israel but in the nations of the world. How does knowing this affect how you think about his wrath and about his justice?
6. In Jeremiah 9:24, God describes himself as "the LORD who practices steadfast love, justice, and righteousness in the earth" (ESV). Do you tend to think of God's justice more as in the past, present day, or time to come? Explain why. How does Jeremiah 9:24 support or challenge how you think of God's justice?

CLOSING PRAYER

Spend some time praying for one another's growth if you're in a group, or for yourself if you're doing this study on your own. Consider what you hope to gain, and ask the Lord to help you grow in that way.

DAY 1

WHAT DOES THE TEXT SAY?

For three sins of Damascus, even for four, I will not relent.
Because she threshed Gilead with sledges having iron teeth.

AMOS 1:3

PRAY

Lord, would you give me understanding as I study this portion of your Word? Awaken my ears to hear and to be instructed such that the meditations of my heart and the words of my mouth are filled with wisdom from your Word. Teach me now I pray, amen. (from Isaiah 50:4-5)

READ

Amos 1:1–2:5

OBSERVE

The introductory verse of the book of Amos is packed with important information. Consider this verse, Amos 1:1, then answer the following questions.

1. The prophet Amos begins speaking in verse 2. What does he tell us the Lord is doing? How is creation responding?

2. Who are the seven transgressing nations Amos is speaking to in verses 1:3–2:5?

3. What phrase does the prophet Amos use before addressing each nation to let us know that it is the Lord who is speaking?

4. What phrase do we hear the Lord repeat?

5. What other words or themes do you see repeated?

6. Consider the number of times the Lord uses the personal pronoun *I* in saying "I will." How does this aid your thinking about his involvement in his world?

7. How does the language of "transgressions" and "punishment" confirm how you think about God? How does it challenge your thinking?

REFLECT

How have you seen the heart of God in your observations?

DAY 2

WHAT DOES THE TEXT MEAN? PART 1

For three sins of Gaza, even for four, I will not relent.
Because she took captive whole communities and sold them to Edom.

AMOS 1:6

PRAY

Lord, would you awaken my ears to hear truth as you lead me through your Word? You are perfect wisdom, knowledge, and understanding. Please impart all of these by your Spirit today, in Jesus' name, amen. (from Proverbs 9:10)

READ

Amos 1:1–2:5

DEFINING OUR TERMS

What is *justice*?

> ***Justice* in its most basic meaning is about treating people equitably, giving people what they are due.**

Justice in its most basic meaning is about treating people equitably, giving people what they are due, whether punishment, protection, or care. It involves punishment for wrongdoing (retributive justice), but also defending the rights (restorative justice) of the poor and needy—often in Scripture named as the orphans, widows, and immigrants. It is helpful to know that *justice* and *righteousness* are often used in close connection with one another throughout Scripture, at the very least suggesting that doing justice is the expected work of the righteous.

While the judgments on the nations in the book of Amos are certainly retributive in nature, the whole of Scripture deals with restorative justice far more. In understanding the judgments named in this portion of Scripture, we learn what makes the "Lion" roar—what makes the Lord angry and his judgments imminent. And in learning what makes him angry, we also learn what he values, what he is passionate about. We discover that while these judgments may seem harsh, at their core they are God's fierce assertion of the dignity and value of all human life, his unwavering care for those made in his image.

The judgments in the book of Amos represent each nation's disordered love for itself or excessive desire for its own gain at the expense of the dignity and value of all human life. Such excessive desires can be categorized in a word—*idol.*

What is an *idol*?

> **An *idol* is anything used as a functional savior and pursued apart from Yahweh (Israel's covenant God) to satisfy a person's or people's longings.**

An *idol*[1] is anything used as a functional savior and pursued apart from Yahweh (Israel's covenant God) to satisfy a person's or people's longings. The deep idols of our hearts can be thought of as being part of the following categories.

- **Idol of power**—An excessive desire for significance achieved through success, winning, and influence.
- **Idol of control**—An excessive desire for certainty that leads one to attempt to control themselves, their environment, and others around them.
- **Idol of approval**—An excessive desire to please, to get affirmation and acceptance from relationships.
- **Idol of comfort**—An excessive desire for avoidance of pain or stress by seeking freedom from responsibilities, expectations, or anything that might feel unpleasant.

READING THE PROPHETS WELL: ORACLES

Oracles are the legal proceedings of the one true Righteous Judge against an erring people.

The judgments of God recorded in the books of the Prophets (both major and minor) are often presented in literary devices called ***oracles***. Oracles are the legal proceedings of the one true Righteous Judge against an erring people. These devices usually begin with a phrase such as "Thus says the Lord," intended to highlight the fact that the prophet is speaking the very words of Yahweh, Israel's covenant God. We will refer to such a phrase as a *prophetic formula*. The judgments against the nations establish that Yahweh is not only the Righteous Judge of Israel, but of all creation.

The structure of the oracles in the book of Amos are very distinct, and if understood will aid our understanding of the charges being brought against the nations and the nature of their coming judgment. Let's look at the oracle concerning Damascus in Amos 1:3-5 as an example:

Prophetic formula: *"This is what the Lord says."* This phrase makes it clear that the Prophet Amos is speaking the words he was given by the Lord.

"For three sins of Damascus, even for four, I will not relent." This refrain is a statement of the fullness of Damascus' sin and the certainty of God's coming judgment.

Charge: *"Because she threshed Gilead with sledges having iron teeth."* The charge describes the specific way the nation has violated God's law.

Judgment: *"I will send fire on the house of Hazael that will consume the fortresses of Ben-Hadad. I will break down the gate of Damascus; I will destroy the king who is in the Valley of Aven and the one who holds the scepter in Beth Eden."* The judgments are Yahweh's personal statements of retributive justice—how he will judge the actions of the nation.

Resulting Conditions: *"The people of Aram will go into exile to Kir."* These are the resulting conditions from Yahweh's judgments.

Closing Prophetic Formula: *"Says the Lord."* This statement acts almost as a closing quotation mark indicating the end of the Lord's very words spoken through his prophet. You may notice that some oracles will not have a closing prophetic formula.

COMPLETE THE CHART

Complete the first three sections of the chart for the nations named in Amos 1:6-10. The first one is done for you. Take time to locate each nation on the map of Israel and her neighbors to understand where they were located in relation to Israel. Leave the last column blank for now. We will complete it in a later lesson.

EXAMINE

1. How do the details given in the introductory verse shape your understanding of Amos's prophecy as an actual historical event?

Chart for oracles of judgment of the nations in Amos 1:6-10

Nation being Accused "For three sins of . . ."	*Charge Against Them* "Because they have . . ."	*Judgment Given* "So I [the LORD] will . . ."
DAMASCUS (Amos 1:3-5)	Threshed Gilead with sledges of iron	Send a fire upon the house of Hazael; break the gate-bar of Damascus; cut off the inhabitants from the Valley of Aven
GAZA (Amos 1:6-8)		Send fire on the walls of Gaza; destroy the kings of Ashdod and Ashkelon; turn my hand against Ekron
TYRE (Amos 1:9-10)	Sold whole communities of captives to Edom, disregarding a treaty of brotherhood	
EDOM (Amos 1:11-12)	Pursued his brother with a sword and slaughtered the women of the land, because his anger raged continually and his fury flamed unchecked	Send fire on Teman
AMMON (Amos 1:13-15)	Ripped open the pregnant women of Gilead in order to extend his borders	
MOAB (Amos 2:1-3)		Send fire on Moab; destroy her ruler and kill all her officials with him
JUDAH (Amos 2:4-5)	Rejected the law of the LORD and have not kept his decrees; been led astray by false gods, the gods their ancestors followed	

2. How might Amos's ministering in a different area than where he lived have been helpful for him? How might it have been a disadvantage?

Resulting Conditions	*Idols Being Confronted*
Strongholds of Ben-Hadad devoured; inhabitants cut off; the king and people of Syria will go into exile to Kir	Power, Control
Fortresses of Gaza consumed by fire; death of all the Philistines	
Fortresses of Tyre consumed by fire	
Fortresses of Rabbah consumed amid war cries on the day of battle, amid violent winds on a stormy day; her king and officials will go into exile together	
Fortresses of Kerioth consumed; Moab will go down in great tumult amid war cries and the blast of the trumpet	
Fortresses of Jerusalem consumed	

Map of Israel and neighbors

Use the first four columns of the oracles of judgment chart to answer the remaining questions.

1. Nearly all charges against the nations involve crimes against humanity. What common theme do you see in the charges against the nations?

2. Consider the resulting conditions column on the oracles of judgment chart. What is significant about what gets consumed by fire?

REFLECT

Consider which crimes against humanity provoke a strong response for you. Now consider the crimes against humanity for which you could easily change the channel. What does your emotion reveal about what you value highly or value less so?

DAY 3

WHAT DOES THE TEXT MEAN? PART 2

For three sins of Tyre, even for four, I will not relent.
Because she sold whole communities of captives to
Edom, disregarding a treaty of brotherhood.

AMOS 1:9

PRAY

Lord, because perfect wisdom is yours alone, would you impart wisdom as we study your Word? Teach us who you are such that our reverence for you informs how we show up in your world, amen. (from Proverbs 9:10)

READ

Amos 1:1–2:5

COMPLETE THE CHART

Complete the last four sections of the oracles of judgment chart for the nations named in Amos 1:11–2:5. The first one is done for you. Take time to locate each nation on the map of Israel to understand where they were located in relation to Israel. Leave the last column blank for now. We will complete it in a later lesson.

Chart for oracles of judgment of the nations in Amos 1:11–2:5

Nation being Accused "For three sins of . . ."	*Charge Against Them* "Because they have . . ."	*Judgment Given* "So I [the LORD] will . . ."
DAMASCUS (Amos 1:3-5)	Threshed Gilead with sledges of iron	Send a fire upon the house of Hazael; break the gate-bar of Damascus; cut off the inhabitants from the Valley of Aven
GAZA (Amos 1:6-8)		Send fire on the walls of Gaza; destroy the kings of Ashdod and Ashkelon; turn my hand against Ekron
TYRE (Amos 1:9-10)	Sold whole communities of captives to Edom, disregarding a treaty of brotherhood	
EDOM (Amos 1:11-12)	Pursued his brother with a sword and slaughtered the women of the land, because his anger raged continually and his fury flamed unchecked	Send fire on Teman
AMMON (Amos 1:13-15)	Ripped open the pregnant women of Gilead in order to extend his borders	
MOAB (Amos 2:1-3)		Send fire on Moab; destroy her ruler and kill all her officials with him
JUDAH (Amos 2:4-5)	Rejected the law of the LORD and have not kept his decrees; been led astray by false gods, the gods their ancestors followed	

EXAMINE

1. Considering the low social status of shepherds, how might Amos's occupation have affected his message?

Resulting Conditions	*Idols Being Confronted*
Strongholds of Ben-Hadad devoured; inhabitants cut off; the king and people of Syria will go into exile to Kir	Power, Control
Fortresses of Gaza consumed by fire; death of all the Philistines	
Fortresses of Tyre consumed by fire	
Fortresses of Rabbah consumed amid war cries on the day of battle, amid violent winds on a stormy day; her king and officials will go into exile together	
Fortresses of Kerioth consumed; Moab will go down in great tumult amid war cries and the blast of the trumpet	
Fortresses of Jerusalem consumed	

2. Using the oracles of judgment chart, compare Judah's judgment to that of the other nations. How are the charges against Judah different from those against the other nations? What does it say about the relationship of God's law to righteous living? What does it suggest about the seriousness of idolatry?

3. Use the definition of *idols* given on day two to complete the last column of the oracles of judgment chart. Consider the charge brought against each nation and determine what idol might be informing the behavior. The first one is completed for you.

REFLECT

As you learn about the oracles against the nations, what kind of charges do you think Amos might bring against twenty-first century people living in the United States? What idols would he confront?

DAY 4

WHAT DOES THE REST OF SCRIPTURE SAY?

For three sins of Judah, even for four, I will not relent.
Because they have rejected the law of the LORD*.*

AMOS 2:4

PRAY

Lord, open my eyes and show me wonderful things in this portion of Scripture. More than informed, help me be transformed by the renewing of my mind by the power of your Spirit. In Jesus' name, amen. (from Psalm 119:18 and Romans 12:2)

READ

Amos 1:1–2:5

SEARCH THE SCRIPTURES

1. The prophet Zechariah mentions "the earthquake" in Zechariah 14:5. How do we know he is likely referencing the same earthquake as Amos 1:1? Zechariah prophesied nearly two hundred years after Amos. How does Zechariah's mention of the earthquake affect your confidence in the occurrence of the event as historic fact?

2. What is the relationship between the threshing with sledges of iron, or cruelty, in Amos 1:3 and oppression? Consider the following passages.

He will rescue them from ***oppression*** *and violence, for precious is their blood in his sight.* **(Psalm 72:14)**	*But your eyes and your heart are set only on dishonest gain, on shedding innocent blood and on* ***oppression*** *and extortion.* **(Jeremiah 22:17)**	*This is what the Sovereign LORD says: You have gone far enough, princes of Israel! Give up your violence and* ***oppression*** *and do what is just and right. Stop dispossessing my people, declares the Sovereign LORD.* **(Ezekiel 45:9)**	*A people that you do not know will eat what your land and labor produce, and you will have nothing but cruel* ***oppression*** *all your days.* **(Deuteronomy 28:33)**

3. What are some of the actions that are associated with oppression? From these passages, what is the heart of God concerning cruelty and oppression?

4. In Amos 1:6, Gaza took and sold a whole people into slavery to Edom. In Amos 1:9, Tyre also sold captives to Edom and disregarded the "treaty of brotherhood." How does Jeremiah describe the covenant (or treaty) of brotherhood in Jeremiah 34:8-10? Who is the treaty between? How are God's priorities seen in the terms of this covenant?

5. In the oracles of judgment against Israel's neighbors, each of the judgments involve the Lord sending fire upon each nation's area of strength, protection, and self-sufficiency. Consider similar acts of judgment in other passages of Scripture.

I will send fire on Magog and on those who live in safety in the coastlands, and they will know that I am the LORD. **(Ezekiel 39:6)**	*Israel has forgotten their Maker and built palaces; Judah has fortified many towns. But **I will send fire** on their cities that will consume their fortresses.* **(Hosea 8:14)**	*But if you do not obey me to keep the Sabbath day holy by not carrying any load as you come through the gates of Jerusalem on the Sabbath day, then **I will kindle an unquenchable fire** in the gates of Jerusalem that will consume her fortresses.* **(Jeremiah 17:27)**

6. Consider the judgment of the Lord sending fire. How is it similar to the refrain in Amos: "For three sins of . . . even for four, I will not relent." Does the judgment come in response to one unique action or a pattern of behavior? Explain your answer.

7. In some of the judgment oracles, the leaders of the nations are named specifically in the Lord's imminent judgment, i.e., in Amos 1:8: "the one who holds the scepter." How might leaders have a unique role in affecting how people under their leadership are treated equitably? What role might nonleaders play in creating spaces where all people are treated with equity?

REFLECT

Have you ever had anyone in leadership stand up for you to be treated fairly? Have you ever stood up for someone else? What was the outcome?

DAY 5

PRACTICING JUSTICE

Let not the wise man boast in his wisdom, let not the mighty man boast in his might, let not the rich man boast in his riches, but let him who boasts boast in this, that he understands and knows me, that I am the LORD who practices steadfast love, justice, and righteousness in the earth. For in these things I delight, declares the LORD.

JEREMIAH 9:23-24 (ESV)

PRAY

Lord, your Word is a lamp unto my feet and a light unto my path. Send your truth today as a lamp that gives clarity in awareness of the places of influence where I stand, and of the attitudes and motivations of my heart. Send your Word as a light that shows me how to navigate the path ahead to participate in the restorative work you are doing. You are the God who practices steadfast love, justice, and righteousness in the earth. Please show me how to participate in your work of making all things new. In Jesus' name, amen. (from Psalm 119:105 and Jeremiah 9:24)

READ

Amos 1:1–2:5

RESPOND

1. Practicing justice is personal. It is also systemic—it can be embedded within the structures, institutions, and policies of a society, leading to disparities and inequities across groups. We tend to think of it more one way than the other. Do you tend to think of justice as more personal or systemic? Explain why.

2. How might it look for you to think of justice as participating in God's restorative work of practicing justice in the earth?

3. The Lord says of himself in Jeremiah 9 that he is the one who practices justice in the earth. How often do you think of God in this way? What are the barriers in our cultural moment to your seeing him in this way?

4. What are some heart attitudes you identified in the charges against the nations? Choose one that you see at play in the systems surrounding you—where you live, work, and play.

5. Consider what the judgments targeted among the nations—places of perceived strength and self-sufficiency. What are your greatest areas of strength? Where might you most need to be reminded to depend on the Lord?

6. What concerns do you have about surrounding nations? Have you ever thought to pray for them? Why or why not?

PRAY

Gracious Father, you are the One who practices steadfast love, justice, and righteousness in the earth. That includes [insert the system of inequity you have identified]. I often act out of my own self-sufficiency in the area of [insert the system of inequity you have identified]. Help me grow in awareness of my desperate need of you, even in the areas where I feel most sufficient, amen.

WEEK 2
ISRAEL HEARS THE ROAR

He answered, "'Love the Lord your God with all your heart and with all your soul and with all your strength and with all your mind'; and, 'Love your neighbor as yourself.'"

LUKE 10:27

GROUP SESSION INTRODUCTION

In our previous session, we discussed how the Lord's roaring put all the nations of the world on notice that the earth and all its fullness are his domain. In this week's lesson, it is Israel who is the object of the Lord's roar, his imminent judgment.

This is what the LORD says:

"For three sins of Israel,
even for four, I will not relent.
They sell the innocent for silver,
and the needy for a pair of sandals.

They trample on the heads of the poor
as on the dust of the ground
and deny justice to the oppressed." (Amos 2:6-7)

OPENING PRAYER

God of grace, would you give us an awareness of how weak and anemic our efforts at loving our neighbors are without your love flowing through us? Help us to love you with our whole hearts, that we might be better able to love our neighbors with the power of your love at work in us, amen. (from Luke 10:27 and Colossians 1:29)

SCRIPTURE

Read aloud Amos 2:6-16.

VIDEO

Watch this week's video.

GROUP DISCUSSION

1. How do you think Israel was feeling as they heard the judgments against their neighbors? Their neighbors had been cruel toward the poor and denied justice to disadvantaged people groups. How do you think Israel's response changed as similar judgments were being made against them?
2. Jesus speaks to our tendency to see others' faults before our own in his teaching in Matthew 7:3-5, where he says to remove the plank from our own eye so that we might see more clearly how to remove the speck from others' eyes. How might we gain greater clarity of the planks in our eyes—our participation in or indifference toward unjust practices?
3. Do you think of our tendencies toward injustice as more of a knowledge issue or a love issue? Explain why.
4. Can you think of a modern example of "the innocent being sold for silver"?
5. Can you think of examples of the poor being trampled into the dust or treated with cruelty?
6. The Lord reminded Israel of ways he had fought for and rescued them. Are there situations you can point to where you clearly received the Lord's help? How might rehearsing what the Lord has done in your life help you?

CLOSING PRAYER

The apostle Paul teaches in Romans 12:2-3 about our minds being transformed and renewed, and one of the means of such renewal and transformation is the Word of God. It is the renewed and transformed mind that allows us to see ourselves objectively or with sober judgment, with clarity. Spend some time praying for one another if you are in a group, or for yourself if you are doing this study on your own. Ask the Lord for minds that are transformed and renewed through his Word, and for clear vision to see ourselves and the world around us.

DAY 1

WHAT DOES THE TEXT SAY?

For three sins of Israel, even for four, I will not relent.
They sell the innocent for silver, and the
needy for a pair of sandals.

AMOS 2:6

PRAY

Lord, you are the righteous King who upholds the cause of the oppressed and gives food to the hungry. Every act of injustice is an affront to your character. Please teach me your ways of mercy and justice. Give me a heart tender to the cause of the oppressed, ears sensitive to your voice, and feet that rush to the aid of the poor, amen. (from Psalm 146)

READ

Amos 2:6-16

OBSERVE

1. What people group is Israel charged with selling and trampling in verses 6 and 7? How do they treat this demographic?

2. Who does Israel specifically "turn aside" or deny justice to, according to verse 7?

3. In what ways does the Lord recount his faithfulness to Israel in verses 9-10? How has he dealt with their enemies? How did he care for them in the wilderness?

4. How did the Lord provide through their children, according to verse 11?

5. As shown in verse 12, how did Israel treat the Lord's provision?

6. How does the Lord respond in verses 13-16 to Israel's treatment of the poor and the oppressed? Which types of persons are named? What's the significance of those persons?

REFLECT

Consider why the Lord concerns himself with justice for the disadvantaged. Who are those persons around you?

DAY 2

WHAT DOES THE TEXT MEAN? PART 1

They trample on the heads of the poor as on the dust of the ground and deny justice to the oppressed.

AMOS 2:7

PRAY

Lord, you have promised to lead us into all truth by your Spirit. Please teach me your priorities that they might become my priorities, in Jesus' name, amen. (from John 15:26 and 16:13)

READ

Amos 2:6-16

DEFINING OUR TERMS

Who are the oppressed?

The *oppressed* or "the crushed" are those burdened with cruel or unjust impositions or restraints; it also includes those subjected to a burdensome or harsh exercise of authority or power. The word *oppress* generally describes the intimidation and exploitation (with overtones of extortion and violence) of weaker members of the community by those who are stronger.[1]

> **The *oppressed* or "the crushed" are those burdened with cruel or unjust impositions; it also includes the intimidation and exploitation (with overtones of extortion and violence) of weaker members of the community by those who are stronger.**

Amos 2:9-11 deviates from the format we've seen in the oracles against the other nations as the Lord recounts the many ways he had kept his covenant with Israel. He reminds them of his faithfulness in battle against mighty enemies, in delivering them from their oppressors in Egypt, in leading them for forty years through the wilderness, in giving them the land of their enemies, in raising up prophets who warned them and spoke his heart and ways to the people, and in raising up Nazirites to provide an example of faithful living among them. It's clear from these examples that Israel had a

READING THE PROPHETS WELL: UNDERSTANDING JUDGMENT

A consistent theme we considered in the Lord's judgments against the nations was that he came against their areas of strength, self-sufficiency, and power. His judgment against Israel bears a similar theme. He comes against the strong, the mighty, the swift. All the ways that they could use to avoid the impending judgment of the Lord would perish. His impending judgment "on that day" (Amos 2:16) was inevitable.

You may remember that each of the judgments on Israel's neighbors included the Lord sending fire. While the Lord certainly pronounced judgment on Israel, he didn't use the "sending fire" language in their judgment. Some scholars suggest that changing the ending from the expected conclusion of "sending fire" to something different was an intentional literary move to hold the attention of the audience.[2] He continues to speak to Israel in the language of their covenant, which did not include destruction by fire as a consequence of disobedience (see Deuteronomy 28).

What we can be certain of is that each accusation and judgment against Israel and her neighbors is a window into the heart of God—what he loves, what he abhors, what he treasures, what he detests. Wading through the overwhelming messiness of the nations' unrighteousness causes us to long for a righteous remedy that would only be found in Christ. It's only in understanding the depth of the bad news of the judgments that we will be able to understand just how good the good news of God's love toward us through Christ really is. However large the message of judgment that looms over Israel and the nations in our text, the enormity of God's grace, his lovingkindness, is greater by far. God's judgments are never because he takes pleasure in punishing the wicked, but instead that they might turn from wickedness to him in repentance (Ezekiel 18:23).

special relationship with the Lord that brought with it heightened responsibility and expectations of holy living.

EXAMINE

1. How would you have defined being *oppressed* before beginning this study? Did you think of it as a biblical term or as part of a more modern social construct? How does reading it on the pages of Scripture affect how you understand it?

2. Read Amos 2:9-11. In what ways had the Lord demonstrated his faithfulness?

3. The "but" of verse 12 indicates a pivot from the Lord declaring his faithfulness to the way Israel discounted his provision. In what ways does he come against Israel's misuse of power in verses 13-16?

REFLECT

What were your impressions of God's judgments before beginning this study? How has today's lesson challenged or supported your previous views?

DAY 3

WHAT DOES THE TEXT MEAN? PART 2

I also raised up prophets from among your children
and Nazirites from among your youths.

AMOS 2:11

PRAY

Lord, give me a heart tender to your promptings to return to you from every wandering. Thank you that even your judgments prove your kindness toward your creation in calling us to return to our created purpose, living lives that reflect your goodness, faithfulness, and justice, amen. (from Ezekial 18:32 and Isaiah 42:6)

READ

Amos 2:6-16

EXAMINE

1. Look at the oracle of judgment against Israel chart. How do the charges against Israel compare to the other nations? What's the same? What's different?

Chart of the oracle of judgment against Israel in Amos 2:6-16

Nation being Accused "For three sins of . . ."	*Charge Against Them* "Because they have . . ."	*Judgment Given* "So I [the LORD] will . . ."
ISRAEL (Amos 2:6-8, 12-16)	**Amos 2:6-8** Sell the righteous for silver, and the needy for a pair of sandals; trample the head of the poor into the dust; turn aside the way of the afflicted; profane the Lord's holy name through sexual immorality; false worship; abuse of power **Amos 2:12** Made the Nazirites drink wine; commanded the prophets not to prophesy	Punish you for all your iniquities; press you down in your place

2. Consider verses 14-16 to complete the "Resulting Conditions" column of your chart.

3. What areas of strength and self-sufficiency is the Lord coming against in Israel? What idols are being confronted? List them in the "Idols Being Confronted" column of your chart.

REFLECT

Look back at the categories of idols in the chart. Which of these resonate most with you? Is there any correlation to your strengths and the areas that resonate most? Explain.

Resulting Conditions	*Idols Being Confronted*

DAY 4

WHAT DOES THE REST OF SCRIPTURE SAY?

I brought you up out of Egypt and led you forty years in the wilderness.

AMOS 2:10

PRAY

Lord, give us hearts that rehearse the truth of who you are and all the ways you've been faithful to us. Let our remembrance foster humble reliance on your Spirit being at work in us, amen. (from Deuteronomy 8:18 and Colossians 1:29)

READ

Amos 2:6-16

SEARCH THE SCRIPTURES

1. A charge against Israel was that "Honest people (the righteous) who could be trusted to repay eventually, were sold for the silver they owed."[2] What other righteous person in Scripture was sold for silver? Read Matthew 26:14-16. How does this passage shape your thoughts on how the Father views selfish gain at the expense of others?

2. Another charge against Israel was that "the desperately poor (the needy) were enslaved because they could not pay back the insignificant sum they owed for a pair of sandals."[3] How does Scripture address economic inequalities through debt alleviation for the poor? Read Deuteronomy 15:1-2, Matthew 18:23-27, and Nehemiah 5:1-13.

3. How did God's covenant require Israel to treat the poor? Read Deuteronomy 15:7-11. Discuss how Amos 2:6 describes Israel's rebellion against God's covenant.

4. Read the following passages and describe God's heart for the oppressed in each passage: Psalm 103:6 and Psalm 146:7.

5. Scripture repeatedly names certain people groups as the oppressed or the vulnerable and disadvantaged. Identify who those groups are in the following passages.

This is what the LORD Almighty said: "Administer true justice; show mercy and compassion to one another. Do not oppress the widow or the fatherless, the foreigner or the poor. Do not plot evil against each other." **(Zechariah 7:9-10)**	*You shall not oppress a hired worker who is poor and needy, whether he is one of your brothers or one of the sojourners who are in your land within your towns.* **(Deuteronomy 24:14 ESV)**	*But you, God, see the trouble of the afflicted; you consider their grief and take it in hand. The victims commit themselves to you; you are the helper of the fatherless.* **(Psalm 10:14)**	*Religion that is pure and undefiled before God the Father is this: to visit orphans and widows in their affliction.* **(James 1:27 ESV)**

6. Amos 2:12 describes Israel seeking to silence truth by forbidding the prophets to prophesy. Where else in Scripture do we see those opposing truth seeking to silence God's messengers? Read about the following people. Observe in which of these scenarios the opposition was successful.

- Elijah in 1 Kings 19:1-2

- the apostles Peter and John in Acts 4:1-7, 13-18

- the apostle Paul in Acts 14:19-22

- the apostle John in Revelation 1:9

- Jesus in John 11:48, 57

7. In Amos 2:14-16, the Lord comes against the military might of Israel. Why is this so remarkable? Yet why is it just? Again read Deuteronomy 28:1-7, 15, 25.

REFLECT

What about God's character was helpful for you to remember as you searched the Scriptures?

DAY 5

PRACTICING JUSTICE

The LORD works righteousness and justice for all the oppressed.

PSALM 103:6

PRAY

Father, we have not always looked upon the vulnerable with your compassion. Please help us to not only understand your heart for the oppressed, but to be moved to action. Help us participate in your working righteousness and justice for all who are oppressed. In Jesus' name, amen. (from Psalm 103:6)

READ

Amos 2:6-16

RESPOND

1. In Deuteronomy 15:7-11, God's covenant calls for generosity toward the poor, a principle we hear echoed throughout Scripture. What portion of your town or city has disproportionate poverty? Discuss how often you allow yourself to move close to that part of town or what permission you give yourself not to.

2. Scripture repeatedly names the poor, the fatherless, the widow, and the foreigner as vulnerable people groups who require the compassion and care of their neighbors (see Zechariah 7:9-10; Deuteronomy 24:14; Psalm 10:14; James 1:27). What other disadvantaged people groups might we include today? What do each of these commands teach us about God's priorities?

3. In Amos 2:12, we learn that Israel commanded the prophets—the carriers of the very words of God—not to prophesy. We considered other passages such as John 11 where the truth of God's Word was similarly opposed. Read again John 11:48 and describe the motivation for silencing truth. What idols of the heart are at play?

4. Why should it not be surprising that the Lord came against Israel's military might in Amos 2:14-16? Consider the covenant promises of Deuteronomy 28:1-7, 15, 25. How might you misunderstand the heart of God if you did not know his covenant promises to Israel? Knowing the covenant promises, how does it shape how you understand the heart of God?

5. Name one way you can move toward the vulnerable in your city, town, or neighborhood this week.

6. What idol (power, control, approval, comfort) is most likely to hinder your ability to be a restorative presence in your neighborhood or city? What might your hesitation reveal that you are doubting about the Lord's character?

PRAY

Lord, your heart is so tender toward those who are disadvantaged, impoverished, mistreated. Forgive us where we lack compassion toward those you care so deeply for, and motivate us to participate in the work you are doing right now in the earth through steadfast love, justice, and righteousness. Help us tear down the idols of our hearts until you reign there unrivaled forever, amen.

SUPREME AND FAMILY COURT · STATE OF NEW YORK
320
330

WEEK 3
YOU ONLY HAVE I KNOWN

You yourselves have seen what I did to Egypt,
and how I carried you on eagles' wings and brought you to myself.
Now if you obey me fully and keep my covenant, then out of all
nations you will be my treasured possession.
Although the whole earth is mine.

EXODUS 19:4-5

GROUP SESSION INTRODUCTION

Last week we discussed Israel hearing the roar of the Lord's judgment as the other nations had heard previously. This week we will discuss God's heart for his covenant people as expressed in his statement "You only have I known" (Amos 3:2 ESV).

> Hear this word, people of Israel, the word the LORD has spoken against you—against the whole family I brought up out of Egypt:
>
> "You only have I chosen
> of all the families of the earth;
> therefore I will punish you
> for all your sins." (Amos 3:1-2)

OPENING PRAYER

God of grace, you have set your love upon your children from the foundation of the world. You love us with an everlasting love, one that endures our many failures. Convince us today of your love for us by your Word and Spirit. In Jesus' name, amen. (See Ephesians 1 and 3:18 and Jeremiah 31:3)

SCRIPTURE

Read aloud Amos 3:1-15.

VIDEO

Watch this week's video.

GROUP DISCUSSION

1. What covenants in modern culture bring with them high expectations of how the parties in covenant are to behave with one another?
2. Read Deuteronomy 6:4-9. How might daily reciting the *shema* have shaped Israel's view of God? Of their neighbors? Of their world?
3. What recitation have you grown up saying from memory (i.e., the Pledge of Allegiance, the Lord's Prayer)? How have these shaped what you currently believe?
4. What truth might it be helpful to rehearse in your heart regularly? How might doing so affect what you believe and how you live?
5. How do the people you converse with regularly support your beliefs? What topics do you discuss? Are there topics that are off-limits?
6. Where do you hear views that are different from yours? How often do you have such conversations? Why might it be important to have your beliefs challenged?
7. Who is God's covenant community today? What might this community recite on a regular basis that affects how they believe and live?

CLOSING REFLECTION

What does it mean to you that the God of the universe boldly declares his love to those in relationship with him? Do you find it difficult to believe or understand? Why or why not?

DAY 1

WHAT DOES THE TEXT SAY?

And I will establish my covenant between me and you and your offspring after you throughout their generations for an everlasting covenant, to be God to you and to your offspring after you.

GENESIS 17:7 (ESV)

PRAY

Lord, your words are powerful enough to uphold the entire universe, yet holy enough to wash us until we are clean. Sanctify, cleanse us now with your truth. Your Word is truth, amen. (from Hebrews 1:3 and John 17:17)

READ

Amos 3:1-15

OBSERVE

1. What familial language do you see in the first two verses?

2. Consider the cause and effect nature of the "therefore" in verse 2. Identify the cause that is being implied. Identify the effect.

3. Consider the rhetorical questions of verses 3-6. What is the expected answer to each question?

4. According to verse 8, what compels the prophet to prophesy?

5. What charges does the Lord bring against Israel in verses 9-10?

6. What word begins the charges against Israel in verse 1 and the judgments against them in verse 13?

7. By what title does the Lord identify himself in verse 13 in the ESV? What does this title reveal about the Lord?

REFLECT

In what ways do you see the church functioning as a family? If you are part of God's family, what is your role? If you are not, what might your role be if you became a part of God's family?

DAY 2

WHAT DOES THE TEXT MEAN? PART 1

For the LORD gives wisdom; from his mouth
come knowledge and understanding.

PROVERBS 2:6

PRAY

Lord, you are the God of all wisdom, knowledge, and understanding. Teach us of all these things in this portion of your Word today, in Jesus' name, amen. (from Proverbs 2)

READ

Amos 3:1-15

DEFINING OUR TERMS

What does it mean that God had *known* Israel?

> ***Know* (*yada*) is an experiential or relational knowledge indicating a "special intimacy" that God enjoys with Israel as a result of the Abrahamic and Mosaic covenants (Genesis 12:3 and 28:14; Exodus 19:4-6).**

The word that Yahweh, Israel's covenant God, used to express how he "knows" Israel is *yada*. We discussed the phrase "You only have I known" as being an expression of an intimate, covenantal kind of knowing and not just mere acquaintance. Israel was daily summoned back to a life of obedience in a call to rehearse the truths of who their God was. This was done through a prayer called the *Shema*.

Based in Deuteronomy 6:4-9, the *Shema* is a daily prayer that was recited by ancient Israelites and is still recited by Jewish people today. The prayer is named for its beginning word *shema*[1] or *hear*. "*Shema* in prophetic contexts typically denotes listening by putting into practice what was spoken."[2]

> ***Shema* (shaw-mah') in prophetic contexts typically denotes listening by putting into practice what was spoken. The *Shema* is also a daily prayer that was recited by ancient Israelites and is still recited by Jewish people today. It is based on Deuteronomy 6:4-9 and begins with the word *shema*.**

What did it mean for Israel to be called to *hear*?

It's striking, then, that both Amos 3:1, which begins the accusations against Israel, and Amos 3:11, which begins the judgments against Israel in this chapter, both begin with *shema*. Starting with such an important word for their culture was a way of emphasizing how they had not listened to their own daily prayers centered around loving God and loving their neighbors.

READING THE PROPHETS WELL: THE LORD OF HOSTS

As Israel's covenant God, he has been the one who has protected them and fought for them (see covenant blessings and curses in Deuteronomy 28). He has been Israel's help in times of battle. And now the God who has fought for them is vowing to fight against them—to bring down their defenses and their strongholds and to plunder their wealth. In verse 3:12, Amos paints a dire picture of what will remain in Israel after its judgment—a fraction, mere remnants, of the prosperity they were enjoying, "the corner of a couch and part of a bed" (ESV).

The name *Lord of Hosts* conjures up imagery of the God who commands armies (hosts) of angels. He is the one who is declaring war on Israel, bringing destruction on their place of false worship, "the altars of Bethel"[3] (Amos 3:14), and their ill-gotten opulence—the winter house, the summer house, the houses of ivory, and the great houses (Amos 3:15 ESV).

REFLECT

Yahweh has been Israel's commander. He has fought for them and carried them safely from bondage in Egypt, as they were being pursued across the Red Sea, and through a number of battles after reaching Canaan. How would hearing the news that the Lord of Hosts was about to punish their transgressions have affected them?

DAY 3

WHAT DOES THE TEXT MEAN? PART 2

Hear this word, people of Israel, the word the LORD has spoken against you—against the whole family I brought up out of Egypt.

AMOS 3:1

PRAY

"Show me your ways, LORD, teach me your paths. Guide me in your truth and teach me, for you are God my Savior, and my hope is in you all day long" (Psalm 25:4-5).

READ

Amos 3:1-15

EXAMINE

Verse 3 begins a series of rhetorical questions, a series of actions that are followed by a certain result. The Lord is announcing the certainty that Israel's evil actions will be followed by his righteous judgments—his justice. The rhetoric seems to suggest that it is absurd and not the natural order of things to think divine action won't follow their rebellion.

1. How might Israel have experienced the Lord's assertion to them: "You only have I known of all the families of the earth" (Amos 3:2 ESV)? Consider where they are and what they've heard before this.

2. How has Israel acquired her wealth according to verses 9-10? Considering what you have learned about Israel's covenant with God, why is this accusation troubling?

3. The Lord not only punishes Israel, but he goes after her idols. What does he say about them in verses 14-15? How might this have been received in a time of such great prosperity?

4. In verse 11, the prophet Amos predicts the coming Assyrian invasion of 722 BC. What idols of Israel did he also confront? (You may find the oracles chart helpful here.) What consistent theme have you noticed between Israel's God and idols?

5. Read verse 12 and consider what metaphor Israel would have used to describe God before Amos's message, and what metaphor Amos is using to describe him here. How shocking would this have been to Israel?

REFLECT

Consider some of the metaphors that Scripture uses for God: Shepherd, Father, King. How do you most often think about God?

DAY 4

WHAT DOES THE REST OF SCRIPTURE SAY?

PRAY

Oh Lord, "is not your word like fire and like the hammer that breaks the rock into pieces?" Send your word now to burn away error and break up the stony ground of our hearts. Reorient us until you are our true and deepest love, amen. (from Jeremiah 23:29 and Matthew 13:20-22)

READ

Amos 3:1-15

SEARCH THE SCRIPTURES

1. Look at 1 Samuel 5:1-5. How does this passage demonstrate the Lord's disdain for idolatry?

2. Consider the following exclusive claims of Israel's covenant God. Based on these claims, who does Israel know him to be?

In the beginning God created the heavens and the earth. **(Genesis 1:1)**	*The Lord, the Lord, a God merciful and gracious, slow to anger, and abounding in steadfast love and faithfulness.* **(Exodus 34:6 ESV)**	*Now therefore, if you will indeed obey my voice and keep my covenant, you shall be my treasured possession among all peoples, for all the earth is mine.* **(Exodus 19:5 ESV)**	*You yourselves have seen what I did to the Egyptians, and how I bore you on eagles' wings and brought you to myself.* **(Exodus 19:4 ESV)**

3. Consider the commands of Israel's God. Based on these commands, discuss why Israel's idolatry is such an afront to him.

You shall have no other gods before me. **(Exodus 20:3)**	*Hear, O Israel: The Lord our God, the Lord is one. You shall love the Lord your God with all your heart and with all your soul and with all your might.* **(Deuteronomy 6:4-5 ESV)**	*And all these blessings shall come upon you and overtake you, if you obey the voice of the Lord your God.* **(Deuteronomy 28:2 ESV)**	*But remember the Lord your God, for it is he who gives you the ability to produce wealth, and so confirms his covenant, which he swore to your ancestors, as it is today.* **(Deuteronomy 8:18)**

4. Read 1 Kings 12:25-30 to understand why King Jeroboam established rival shrines, false worship centers including the "altars of Bethel." How significant, then, was it that Amos was reading God's oracles in this place?

5. Read Amos 3:14 and consider how the Lord intends to punish the altars of Baal. Why is this significant? Compare these actions with what is done to the idol in 1 Samuel 5:1-5. What's consistent in both passages? What's different?

REFLECT

How might you explain the benefits of exclusive loyalty to Israel's God in today's culture?

DAY 5
PRACTICING JUSTICE

Dear children, keep yourselves from idols.

1 JOHN 5:21

PRAY

Father, we have not always looked on the vulnerable with your compassion. Please help us to not only understand your heart for the oppressed but to be moved to action. Help us participate in working your righteousness and justice for all who are oppressed. In Jesus' name, amen. (from Psalm 103:6)

READ

Amos 3:1-15

RESPOND

1. How often do you think about the idols of your heart? How comfortable have you become with them?

2. John Calvin is known for saying that "our hearts are idol factories." How does our propensity to have idols inform how you think about your own?

3. Think about how you talk about any underlying excessive desire for power, control, approval, or comfort. Do you excuse it as being "just how you are"? Where have you diminished the seriousness of the idols of your heart?

4. What "you-only-have-I-known" types of relationships do you have? How might those close relationships aid you in growing in awareness of the outward expressions of your heart idols? How might you offer similar accountability to those in close relationship with you?

5. How might you pray differently with a heightened awareness of your idols? How might it look for you to regularly invite the Lord of Hosts to fight against the idols of your heart? Such a prayer might heighten your focus and embolden you to be more other-centered.

PRAY

Gracious Father, as prone as our hearts are to making idols, you are more prone to pursue us for our good and your glory. Would you make us tender to your pursuits and soften our hearts to you such that you alone are Lord of our lives? Thank you for new mercies applied to us this day, amen.

Downtown
Heliport
Evacuation Day
TRUCK
ROUTE
LOCAL
896

WEEK 4
RETURN TO THE LORD

Let the wicked forsake their ways and the unrighteous their thoughts. Let them turn to the Lord, and he will have mercy on them, and to our God, for he will freely pardon.

ISAIAH 55:7

GROUP SESSION INTRODUCTION

Last week we discussed God's heart for his covenant people—"You only have I known"—and how that special relationship brought with it special responsibility. In this week's lesson, Amos calls out the "cows of Bashan," the self-indulgent women of the ruling class in Israel, for their exploitation of those in need.

> Hear this word, you cows of Bashan on Mount Samaria,
>   you women who oppress the poor and crush the needy
>   and say to your husbands, "Bring us some drinks!"
> The Sovereign Lord has sworn by his holiness:
>   "The time will surely come
> when you will be taken away with hooks,
>   the last of you with fishhooks. . . .
> I gave you empty stomachs in every city
>   and lack of bread in every town,
>   yet you have not returned to me,"
>   declares the Lord. (Amos 4:1-2, 6)

OPENING PRAYER

Gracious Father, far too many times we have rejected your invitation to come to you. We find new ways to avoid your presence when you alone can fully satisfy us. Please give us ears tuned to your voice and hearts that long for your presence as much as you long to draw near. Draw us back to yourself again and again until we are satisfied in you alone. It's in the precious name of Jesus we ask, amen. (from Matthew 11:28 and Psalm 107:9)

SCRIPTURE

Read aloud Amos 4:1-13.

VIDEO

Watch this week's video.

GROUP DISCUSSION

1. How might this lesson challenge you in the way you think about luxurious indulgences?
2. How might this lesson challenge you in the way you think about hardship? Have you ever considered a personal hardship a severe mercy from God?
3. Does this passage (Amos 4) equate wealth with evil? Consider how wealth was gained (4:1) and how it was used (4:4-5). What verse(s) in the text might help you think rightly about wealth?
4. According to verses 4-5, Israel performed the acts of worship, including bringing their sacrifices, regularly tithing, and giving an offering. Why then was their worship not pleasing to God?
5. Read Matthew 23:23-24. Discuss with your group what matters of justice, mercy, and faithfulness you may need to attend to.

CLOSING REFLECTION

Ask the Lord to give you a vision for how he would have you attend to matters of justice, mercy, and faithfulness in your context.

DAY 1

WHAT DOES THE TEXT SAY?

Jerusalem, Jerusalem, you who kill the prophets and stone those sent to you, how often I have longed to gather your children together, as a hen gathers her chicks under her wings, and you were not willing.

MATTHEW 23:37

PRAY

Precious Father, from the first day sin separated our first parents from you in the Garden, you have pursued us. And in the climax of your pursuit, you sent your only Son. Cause us to know and respond to your pursuit in loving obedience to the truths of your Word. In Christ's name we pray, amen. (from Genesis 3 and John 3:16)

READ

Amos 4:1-13

OBSERVE

1. What weighty word begins the message of chapter four? Who is being addressed?

2. What are they being charged with in verse 1? Who is being harmed?

3. What words in verses 2 and 3 give imagery for how Israel's exile to Assyria will look?

4. In legal proceedings, oaths are used to swear by something higher than ourselves. Who does the Lord swear by in verse 2? Consider the significance.

5. How many times do you see the prophetic formula "declares the LORD" announcing the voice of God? What other phrase do you see repeated in verses 6-11?

6. The personal pronoun *I* used in conjunction with "declares the Lord" signals divine speech and action. Write down the actions the Lord declares he's taken in verses 6-11.

7. "Therefore" in verse 12 suggests that the reasons for the coming action have been given. What are the resulting actions found in verses 12-13?

REFLECT

Consider an area of suffering in your life. Are you able to identify God's mercy in it? If not, ask him to show you his goodness even amid suffering.

DAY 2

WHAT DOES THE TEXT MEAN? PART 1

I gain understanding from your precepts;
therefore I hate every wrong path.

PSALM 119:104

PRAY

Lord, you are the God of all wisdom, knowledge, and understanding. Teach me all of these things in this portion of your Word today—in Jesus' name, amen. (from Proverbs 2)

READ

Amos 4:1-13

DEFINING OUR TERMS

The prophetic books of Scripture communicate many ideas through vivid poetry and often use repetition in poetry to drive home key ideas. *Parallelism* is a literary device used in poetry that repeats the same sentiment with slightly different phrasing for emphasis. We saw it as early as verse 2 in chapter one of Amos: "The LORD roars from Zion" (phrase 1) and "thunders from Jerusalem" (phrase 2). Each phrase attests to the same reality of God's power and imminent judgment, but using different wording.

> ***Parallelism* is a literary device used in poetry that repeats the same sentiment with slightly different phrasing for emphasis.**

We see more parallelism in verse 1 of chapter four when Amos charges the "cows of Bashan" with "oppress[ing] the poor" (charge 1) and "crush[ing] the needy" (charge 2). *Oppressing* and *crushing* are synonymous terms used to draw great emphasis to the egregious enjoyment of the ill-gotten gains by the ruling class women of Israel. The poor and needy had been crushed to fund their luxurious lifestyle. The prophet uses parallelism in poetry to underscore this truth.

What does it mean for Israel to be called to *return* to the Lord?

Return (_shuv_) is to turn back to God, repent.

It's surprising to hear the haunting refrain, "yet you did not return to me" (ESV), echoed throughout chapter four. The actions the Lord took to woo them back are not what we would immediately think of as ways to regain someone's affections! He gives them hardship: hunger, failed crops, thirst—all difficulties associated with covenant unfaithfulness. Providing these specific hardships was meant to magnify Israel's unfaithfulness and call them back to faithful relationship with their covenant God (see Deuteronomy 28:15-68).

READING THE PROPHETS WELL: THE ROLE OF THE PROPHET

The prophets of Scripture are often thought of as odd characters as a result of the tasks they carry out as God's messengers to his people. For example, Ezekiel ate a scroll and prophesied to dry bones. Hosea married a prostitute and named his children strange names. As isolated acts, these events were certainly strange, but as a part of a broader narrative, they were lived-out object lessons expressing the heart of God to an erring people.

The call to repentance was often the cry of the prophet, an urgent plea for God's people to return to him through covenant faithfulness. We hear the chilling refrain echoed throughout Amos 4, "yet you did not return to me" (ESV), echoing Israel's repeated opportunities and failures to repent. More than odd characters with weird behaviors, the prophets stood in the very place of God, echoing his voice and repeatedly calling his people back to his heart.

REFLECT

What was God's desired response to the hardships he "gave" to Israel? Understanding that hardships come from various conditions in our lives—our sin, our righteousness, and sometimes the sin of others—how does this call to return to the Lord in hardship shape how we are to think about the hardships in our lives?

DAY 3

WHAT DOES THE TEXT MEAN? PART 2

Deal with your servant according to your love
and teach me your decrees.

PSALM 119:124

PRAY

Father, in your lovingkindness, please teach me your ways that I might worship you more fully, in spirit and in truth, amen. (from Psalm 119:124 and John 4:24)

READ

Amos 4:1-13

EXAMINE

The language of Amos 4:2 invokes a divine oath formula: "The LORD God has sworn by his holiness" (ESV). When taking an oath, the oath-taker swears by something higher than himself, so it's striking that the God of Israel swears by himself, affirming that there is no one higher. He swears that an enemy will violently storm and capture the city, taking Israel from their land fastened to ropes with hooks and forcing them out of the city. The cruel nature of their exit wouldn't allow for a dignified departure through exits in the gate but would instead harshly force them through mere breaches in the wall sustained from the attack.[4]

This prophecy was fulfilled in the Assyrian exile of 722 BC. Assyria was a northern Mesopotamian area centered on the Tigris River. Its most significant period of prominence was 1000 to 612 BC when it conquered all of the Near East, including Israel.[5] Assyria's capture of Israel both validated God's promised judgment and definitively established Amos as an authentic prophet of God, since a prophet was proven authentic by the fulfillment of his prophecies (Deuteronomy 18:22).

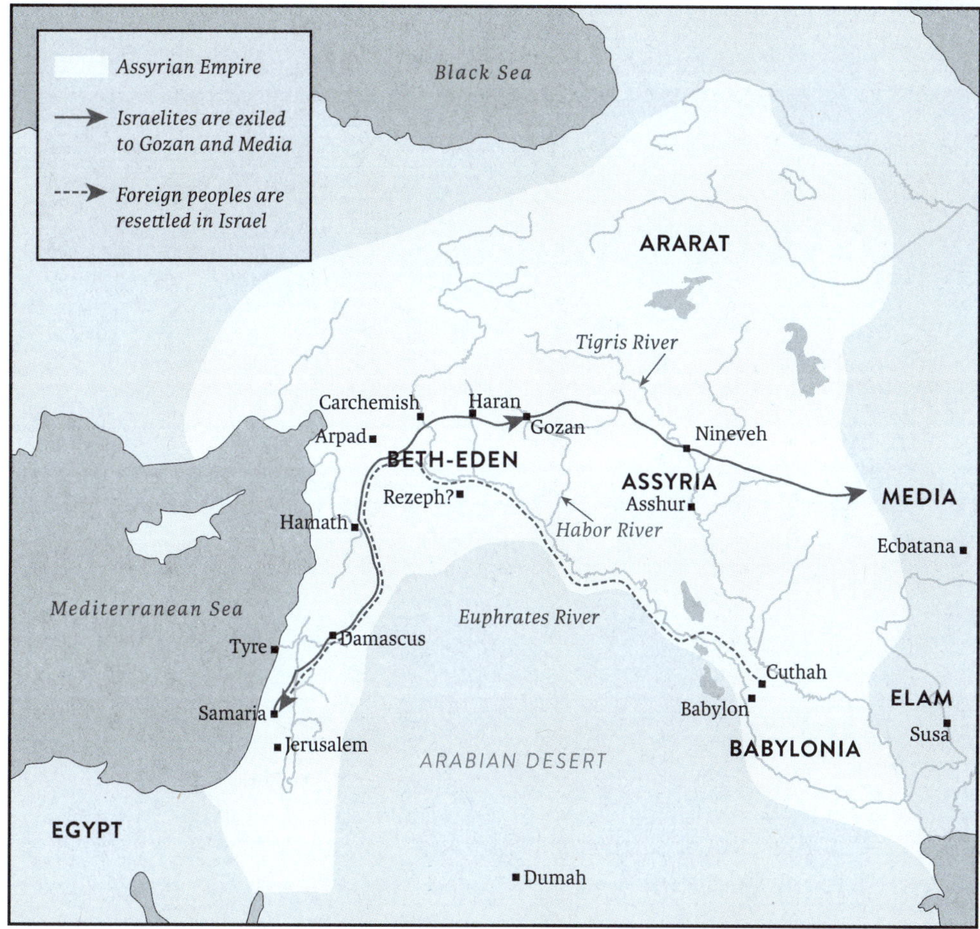

Map of Assyrian Empire

1. We've looked at the significance of God swearing by his holiness. What would Israel think of such a vow?

2. Given the severity of the message, how tempted might Israel have been to dismiss it? At this particular juncture, how important would it have been for Israel to know that the prophet was actually speaking the words of God and not his own?

"DOING WORSHIP"

In verses 4 and 5, the prophet describes the elements of worship happening at Bethel and Gilgal, the cultic worship centers of Israel. The people delighted in the giving of tithes, bringing their offerings, and making sacrifices, all elements associated with faithful worship. Yet Amos concludes that their worship multiplied transgressions against the Lord. It was an offense to him. God's people were "doing worship" as far as all the prescribed actions went, but their hearts were far from him. The evidence was in how they treated their neighbors. Their living proved that their worship was empty.

To worship the God of Israel was to love him more than their comfort, more than their possessions, more than their preferences, and to have a life centered around God and God alone. Worship was never meant to be restricted to one day, but was to be a lifestyle of communion and repentance flowing out as love for neighbors. Israel's temple practices were devoid of any such authenticity. They were merely "doing worship."

On the heels of highlighting the many ways Israel had failed to return to their God, verse 13 concludes the chapter with a re-introduction of Israel's God, almost as if they had never known him. God reminds Israel that he is the mighty King of all creation, sovereign even over man's thoughts, night and day, and the earth's highest heights. He declares himself the fierce commander of the army of angels. He was the One who had fought for them but is now vowing to fight against them, and it's not remotely a fair fight. It is a just one, however, because Israel had repeatedly broken covenant with the God who longed for them to be his people and for him to be their God.

3. Why was the Lord displeased with Israel's worship? In what ways were they "multiplying transgressions"?

4. How often do you think of love of neighbor as being part of authentic worship?

5. How might Israel feel as a covenant breaker to hear God describe his authority, power, and military might?

REFLECTION

If love of neighbor is an outward expression of authentic worship to God—and it is—how would you describe the authenticity of your worship? Ask the Lord to help you see with clarity.

DAY 4

WHAT DOES THE REST OF SCRIPTURE SAY?

May my tongue sing of your word,
for all your commands are righteous.

PSALM 119:172

PRAY

Lord, teach us to study the whole counsel of your Word that we might more fully understand your heart, amen. (from Acts 20:27)

READ

Amos 4:1-13

SEARCH THE SCRIPTURES

1. Read Isaiah 53:4-6 foretelling of Jesus' crucifixion. How does Jesus relate with the oppressed—the crushed—here?

2. Read 2 Kings 18:13-16 and Isaiah 36:1. What king of Assyria would capture Judah, twenty-one years after Assyria took Israel captive?

3. Read Isaiah 10:5-6. What role does Assyria play in God's sovereign plan for Israel and Judah?

4. Based on the passages below, how would you describe God's view of the relationship between authentic worship and love of neighbor?

These people come near to me with their mouth and honor me with their lips, but their hearts are far from me. Their worship of me is based on merely human rules they have been taught. **(Isaiah 29:13)**	*Woe to you, teachers of the law and Pharisees, you hypocrites! You give a tenth of your spices—mint, dill and cumin. But you have neglected the more important matters of the law—justice, mercy and faithfulness. You should have practiced the latter, without neglecting the former.* **(Matthew 23:23)**	*So if you are offering your gift at the altar and there remember that your brother has something against you, leave your gift there before the altar and go. First be reconciled to your brother, and then come and offer your gift.* **(Matthew 5:23-24 ESV)**	*Even though you make many prayers, I will not listen; your hands are full of blood. Wash yourselves; make yourselves clean; remove the evil of your deeds from before my eyes; cease to do evil, learn to do good; seek justice, correct oppression; bring justice to the fatherless, plead the widow's cause.* **(Isaiah 1:15-17 ESV)**

5. Consider the role of the prophet in each of the following passages. What is their message? What are they communicating about the heart of God?

"Yet even now," declares the LORD, "return to me with all your heart, with fasting, with weeping, and with mourning; and rend your hearts and not your garments." Return to the LORD your God, for he is gracious and merciful, slow to anger, and abounding in steadfast love; and he relents over disaster. **(Joel 2:12-13 ESV)**	*Therefore say to them, Thus declares the LORD of hosts: Return to me, says the LORD of hosts, and I will return to you, says the LORD of hosts.* **(Zechariah 1:3 ESV)**	*Come, let us return to the LORD; for he has torn us, that he may heal us; he has struck us down, and he will bind us up.* **(Hosea 6:1 ESV)**	*From the days of your fathers you have turned aside from my statutes and have not kept them. Return to me, and I will return to you, says the LORD of hosts.* **(Malachi 3:7 ESV)**

REFLECT

Considering that God's principles have not changed, what principle do you see reflected in today's reading that you need to remember?

DAY 5

PRACTICING JUSTICE

I rise before dawn and cry for help; I have put my hope in your word.

PSALM 119:147

PRAY

Father, increase our awareness of the ways we fail to see and love those made in your image, and replace the guilt that would weigh us down and destroy us. Cause us to drink deeply from your grace and pour it out liberally on others. In Christ's name we pray, amen. (from Psalm 32:5 and Romans 5:2)

READ

Amos 4:1-13

RESPOND

1. What are the places of hardship in your life that you've allowed to drive you toward doubt and disbelief instead of to the God who loves you?

2. Where might we experience a disconnect in how we live and the human costs associated with our standard of living? Consider the food you eat, the clothes you wear, and so on.

3. Consider the term *essential workers* that emerged during pandemic times. Why were essential workers all of a sudden being celebrated? Does the same gratitude and concern remain for them? Why or why not?

4. What people groups would you describe as economically disadvantaged in your context? Are there people groups who benefit from others' state of poverty? If so, who are those groups?

5. What comforts do you gravitate toward in times of trouble?

6. What challenges drive you toward self-soothing (i.e., food, shopping, marathon watching TV)? How might it look to turn to God when you're tempted to turn to earthly comfort?

REFLECT

Lord, give me eyes to see the poor and needy, those who are disadvantaged in ways I haven't considered. Please don't allow me to be satisfied with my own comforts without considering the strain of others. If I am benefiting from someone else's impoverishment, please reveal that to me. Help me to care more about loving my neighbor than I care about my own comfort. Thank you for the sacrifice of Christ who modeled this kind of love for us. Please love my neighbor through me, amen.

THE CHARL ESTON
B
WOW
URBAN REN EWAL ?
J
P
X
E
SOUL AT THE CENTER
1947
1 O
R A
M
CU LT URE
LOVE
HOM AGE
XX
SAN JUAN HILL
X

WEEK 5
LET JUSTICE ROLL DOWN

When a foreigner resides among you in your land, do not mistreat them. The foreigner residing among you must be treated as your native-born. Love them as yourself, for you were foreigners in Egypt. I am the LORD your God.

LEVITICUS 19:33-34

GROUP SESSION INTRODUCTION

In our last session we heard the haunting refrain "yet you did not return to me" that the Lord uttered to Israel, indicating his severe mercies intended to drive them back to his arms and their refusal to return. In this lesson, we will hear the third and final sermon from Amos beginning with the word *shema* or *hear*: "Hear this word that I take up over you in lamentation, O house of Israel" (Amos 5:1 ESV), as the Lord himself weeps over Israel's plight.

Hear this word, Israel, this lament I take up concerning you:

"Fallen is Virgin Israel,
never to rise again,
deserted in her own land,
with no one to lift her up."
(Amos 5:1-2)

OPENING PRAYER

Father, open our eyes to see wonderful truths about who you are in this portion of your Word. Break our hearts for what breaks yours and move us toward compassion for our neighbor, in Jesus' name, amen. (from Psalm 119:18 and 1 Peter 3:8)

SCRIPTURE

Read aloud Amos 5:1-27.

VIDEO

Watch this week's video.

GROUP DISCUSSION

1. Discuss the destruction of San Juan Hill and the building of Lincoln Center. What are the pros and cons of this past building project? What parts of this situation would you call good and right and what parts (if any) would you call unjust? Is justice satisfied in the Lincoln Center creating a mural to acknowledge the former residents of the neighborhood? Why or why not?
2. How would it have looked for you to be a good neighbor to Mr. Tony Fongyit, the seventy-four-year-old Trinidadian owner of Scoops Ice Cream Parlor in Brooklyn, New York, mentioned in the introductory video? How might your actions have served the neighborhood? How might they have inconvenienced you? How might practicing justice look for the developer who bought Mr. Tony's building?
3. Urban renewal initiatives generally serve to improve the physical and economic aspects of urban areas, but often at the expense of current residents who are priced out of occupying the renovated spaces. Where have you seen urban renewal initiatives near where you live? What's your initial response when seeing them? Have you considered what happened to the original owners? Are they still there or have they been displaced?
4. How difficult is it for you to imagine how flourishing could look for those being treated unjustly? Who might be involved in a solution? What small thing could you do to be a part of a solution?
5. Do you know of anyone who has been displaced or deported? How did you know them? How might you be a good neighbor to a displaced/deported person or the family they leave behind?
6. Let's consider the hiring of a refugee (someone fleeing from threat of imminent harm) or an illegal immigrant to perform cheap labor. Would this be an injustice? Why or why not? How might Scripture inform how we think about such practices (see Leviticus 19:33-34)?

CLOSING PRAYER

Lord, give us courage as we invite your Spirit to examine the nooks and crannies of our hearts. Thank you that when you convict us of offenses, you will never condemn us. Wash us with the truth of your Word until you see your reflection in us, amen.

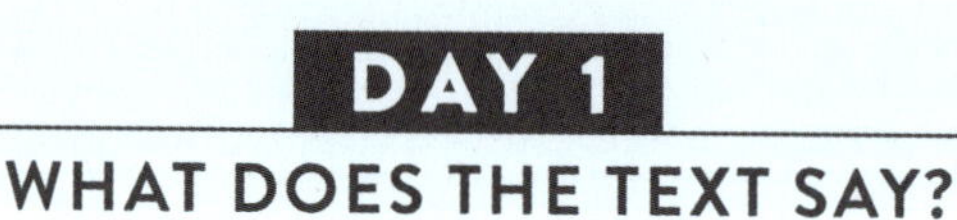

DAY 1
WHAT DOES THE TEXT SAY?

This is what the Lord Almighty says:

"Consider now! Call for the wailing women to come; send for the most skillful of them. Let them come quickly and wail over us till our eyes overflow with tears and water streams from our eyelids."

JEREMIAH 9:17-18

PRAY

Lord, teach us to name the brokenness of our world and run toward it with the truth of your gospel, the only true and living hope. Teach us to weep with those who weep when things are not as they should be, and give us the courage to be agents of restoration by your grace—in Christ's name we pray, amen. (from 1 Peter 1:3 and Romans 12:15)

READ

Amos 5:1-27

OBSERVE

1. What does verse 3 say about the number in which Israel "marches out"? What about the number she will have left?

2. What is Israel exhorted to do in both verses 5 and 6?

3. How many times do you see *weeping, lamenting,* or *wailing* in this chapter? Where are the places of wailing that are named?

4. Consider verses 14-16 in the ESV translation. How many times do you see "Lord" or "God of hosts" language used?

5. Consider the commands concerning good and evil in verses 14 and 15. What are the stated consequences of a right relationship with good and evil?

6. How many times does the phrase "day of the LORD" get repeated in verses 18-20?

7. How does the Lord regard Israel's worship elements listed in verses 21-23? What does he demand instead of their empty worship in verse 24?

REFLECT

In what area of your life might the Lord be inviting you to seek him and live?

DAY 2

WHAT DOES THE TEXT MEAN? PART 1

To God belong wisdom and power;
counsel and understanding are his.

JOB 12:13

PRAY

Lord, you are the God of all wisdom, knowledge, and understanding. Please grant us all of these as we study your Word today—in Jesus' name, amen. (from Job 12:13)

READ

Amos 5:1-27

DEFINING OUR TERMS

What does it mean to "turn justice to wormwood" (verse 7 ESV)?

Justice, or *mishpat* (mish-pawt'), means giving people what they are due, whether punishment, protection, or care.[1] Wormwood is a bitter-tasting, poisonous plant here indicating that justice has been poisoned or perverted.

> ***Justice* (*mishpat*) is giving people what they are due, whether punishment, protection, or care.**

Righteousness is often used in close connection with justice, as it is the act of living justly. *Righteousness, tsedaqah* (tse-daw-kaw'), is being just. It's the day-to-day living in which a person conducts all relationships in family and society with fairness, generosity, and equity.[2]

> ***Righteousness* (*tsedaqah*) is being just; it's the day-to-day living in which a person conducts all relationships in family and society with fairness, generosity, and equity.**

What does it mean to be "skilled in lamentation" (verse 16 ESV)?

In the ancient Near East, wailing women or professional mourners were a fixture at Jewish funerals. According to the *Mishnah* (a collection of Jewish oral traditions): "Even a poor man shall bring no fewer than two flutes and one wailing woman," which meant that a husband was obligated to procure a woman "skilled in lamentation" or a professional mourner for his wife's funeral.[3]

> ***Lamentation*, or *qinah* (kee-naw'), is a dirge (as accompanied by beating the breasts or on instruments); a liturgical response to the reality of suffering that engages God in the context of pain and trouble.[4]**

While there were those who mourned professionally, responding to suffering through lament was also an important part of Israel's corporate worship. Amos 5 demonstrates that lament wasn't Israel's idea. Their God was a God who lamented over the brokenness of his world and invited his people to weep over what was not as it was supposed to be. It is God himself who is weeping over Israel's willful disobedience and unwillingness to return to his heart. He laments as though her demise has already happened.

READING THE PROPHETS WELL: THE DAY OF THE LORD

The "day of the LORD" refers to the end times, a day when Christ returns and brings both judgment to the wicked and deliverance and restoration to the righteous. The "day of the LORD" is an indefinite period of time of divine activity, but it is always an imminent event. Among the Old Testament prophets, Amos is the first to use the expression.[5]

According to Amos's address in verse 18, Israel seems to be joyfully anticipating the day of the Lord, believing that Yahweh will appear as a warrior to defeat their enemies on that day. Amos instead describes the dire conditions that would accompany the Lord's return—a day of gloom and darkness. The language used in verse 17 of Yahweh "passing through" their midst harkens to Exodus 12 where Yahweh "passes through" Egypt to slay their firstborn.[6]

EXAMINE

1. Have you ever seen a child watch their parent cry? What do you think it was like for Israel to know that God was weeping over them?

2. How does the Lord describe Israel in ways that are contrary to his promised covenant blessings?

3. What phrase does the Lord use that proves he doesn't want Israel's downfall? (Hint: He repeats it.)

REFLECT

How do you imagine Israel felt hearing the prophet Amos essentially officiate their funeral while they were yet alive and prospering? How does it challenge you to think about financial prosperity and spiritual health?

DAY 3

WHAT DOES THE TEXT MEAN? PART 2

My heart says of you, "Seek his face!" Your face, Lord, I will seek.

PSALM 27:8

PRAY

"I seek you with all my heart; do not let me stray from your commands" (Psalm 119:10).

READ

Amos 5:1-27

EXAMINE

Instead of proceeding from evil to evil as they have done, the Lord cautions them to instead "hate evil, and love good, and establish justice in the gate" (verse 15 ESV).

The city gate is where business transactions would have happened. Establishing justice at the gate is a call to do justice in their business practices and economic systems. Paul picks up on this concept of hating evil and loving good in Romans 12:9, saying, "Love must be sincere. Hate what is evil; cling to what is good." Our abhorrence of the evils of injustice and cruelty is not to be just an internal disdain. It necessarily means actively hating evil and actively clinging to what is good in both word and deed.

The word *justice* (*mishpat*) occurs more than two hundred times in the Old Testament and is often used with and closely linked to *tsedaqah*, the word for *righteousness* or being just. Like the prophets often do, Amos calls Israel back to what is surely expected of a nation in covenant with Yahweh—justice and righteousness. What Amos is calling for here is not just a slight trickle of justice, an afterthought, an add-on. What he's calling for instead is for justice that flows like a mighty stream from the heart of God through the lives of his people into the world around them. A justice so pervasive that it impacts everything they touch. Pastor Tim Keller puts it this way in his book *Generous Justice*: "A true experience of the grace of Jesus Christ inevitably motivates a man or a woman to seek justice in the world."[7] May we all be so gripped by the enormity of grace poured out toward us that we hurry to pour out grace on others, being a restorative presence in every sphere of influence.

1. Consider the powerful flow of a river current alluded to in Amos 5:24. To what kind of justice is the prophet calling Israel? What language shows that this call is not for a one-time event?

2. Read the specific charges against Israel in Amos 5:10-12. What would have been specific ways for them to "hate evil, and love good" (verse 15 ESV)? How easy or hard do you think that would have been?

3. Amos 5:10 references "him who reproves in the gate" (ESV), referring to the older men of the city who decided the cases of those who came to them for justice. But instead of just rulings, they were giving justice to the highest bidder. Where have you seen wealth be an unfair advantage? How have you seen wealth used to alleviate disadvantage?

4. At the height of Israel's prosperity, the Lord is telling them to seek him and live in Amos 5:4-6. Why might a call to seek the Lord be harder to hear in times of prosperity? Whose flourishing is the Lord seeking in calling Israel back to himself?

5. Read Amos 5:8-9. Who is the mighty source of justice represented here? How then are we to think about the commands of verse 24? Whose work is it?

REFLECT

In Amos 5:5, the Lord tells Israel specifically not to seek Bethel and Gilgal, places of false worship and idolatry. If you were having a private conversation with the Lord, what would he tell you not to seek? Consider places in your life that are hard for you to relinquish control, and ask the Lord to help you relinquish fearful control and cling to him there instead.

DAY 4

WHAT DOES THE REST OF SCRIPTURE SAY?

I meditate on your precepts and consider your ways.

PSALM 119:15

PRAY

Lord, as I come to your Word today, help me to meditate on these truths and be changed by them, in Jesus' name, amen. (from Psalm 119:15)

READ

Amos 5:1-27

SEARCH THE SCRIPTURES

1. Consider these Scripture passages that capture the Lord's lament. Describe what he values and what grieves him in each passage.

Hear, O heavens, and give ear, O earth; for the Lord has spoken: "Children have I reared and brought up, but they have rebelled against me. The ox knows its owner, and the donkey its master's crib, but Israel does not know, my people do not understand." **(Isaiah 1:2-3 ESV)**	*I will take up weeping and wailing for the mountains, and a lamentation for the pastures of the wilderness, because they are laid waste so that no one passes through, and the lowing of cattle is not heard; both the birds of the air and the beasts have fled and are gone. I will make Jerusalem a heap of ruins, a lair of jackals, and I will make the cities of Judah a desolation, without inhabitant.* **(Jeremiah 9:10-11 ESV)**	*And he said to them, "My soul is very sorrowful, even to death." . . . And going a little farther, he fell on the ground and prayed that, if it were possible, the hour might pass from him. And he said, "Abba, Father, all things are possible for you. Remove this cup from me. Yet not what I will, but what you will."* **(Mark 14:34-36 ESV)**	*Now from the sixth hour there was darkness over all the land until the ninth hour. And about the ninth hour Jesus cried out with a loud voice, saying, "Eli, Eli, lema sabachthani?" that is, "My God, my God, why have you forsaken me?"* **(Matthew 27:45-46 ESV)**

2. The "day of the Lord" refers to the end times when Christ will return and bring both judgment to the wicked and deliverance and restoration to the righteous. What is being anticipated in the verses listed below? Compare the descriptions to Amos's description in 5:18-20.

Behold, I will send you Elijah the prophet before the great and awesome day of the Lord comes. And he will turn the hearts of fathers to their children and the hearts of children to their fathers. **(Malachi 4:5-6 ESV)**	*The sun will be turned to darkness and the moon to blood before the coming of the great and dreadful day of the Lord.* **(Joel 2:31)**	*The great day of the Lord is near—near and coming quickly. The cry on the day of the Lord is bitter; the Mighty Warrior shouts his battle cry.* **(Zephaniah 1:14)**	*But the day of the Lord will come like a thief, and then the heavens will pass away with a roar, and the heavenly bodies will be burned up and dissolved, and the earth and the works that are done on it will be exposed.* **(2 Peter 3:10 ESV)**

REFLECT

Do you long for the day the Lord returns? If so, what do you look forward to being made right? If not, explain why.

DAY 5

PRACTICING JUSTICE

He has shown you, O mortal, what is good. And what does the LORD require of you? To act justly and to love mercy and to walk humbly with your God.

MICAH 6:8

PRAY

Father, while I may desire to act justly, I'm not always clear on how that should look and sometimes default to doing nothing. You said that if anyone lacks wisdom, they should ask you, and you would give it liberally. Give us the wisdom and courage to act justly such that our compulsion toward neighbor love overwhelms our fears and self-love, amen. (from James 1:5 and Mark 12:30-31)

READ

Amos 5:1-27

RESPOND

1. What does it mean for you that the God who is sovereign over the entire world weeps over its brokenness? Try to imagine God's perspective on your city. What might he lament? What people groups would he weep for?

2. How might it look for you to write a lament for your city? What people groups would you weep for? What situations could you take before the Lord and declare that this is not the way it is supposed to be?

3. Using the instructions below, spend some time over the next week writing your own personal lament.

WRITING YOUR OWN PSALM OF LAMENT

The book of Psalms served as the songbook of Israel with about 40 percent of its psalms being psalms of lament. Lamentation was clearly a regular part of Israel's corporate worship. Only 13-19 percent of the songs in mainline

American church hymnals are songs of lament, which are most often used in funeral services.[8] Most of the songs used in regular worship reflect themes of praise. While songs of praise are essential in worship, an overemphasis on praise can indicate a lack of awareness of suffering and the need for the language of lament to be normalized in the context of corporate worship.

Lament can be thought of as not simply the presentation of a list of complaints, nor merely the expression of sadness over difficult circumstances. More than that, "lament is a liturgical response to the reality of suffering that engages God in the context of pain and trouble."[9] Psalms of lament give voice to such suffering, inviting us to express our deepest griefs and showing us a way to rightly process our suffering and the suffering of others. The Psalms contain the full range of human emotion and provide us "a God-authored script by which the full gamut of human experience can be expressed."[10] The expression of lament is often the vehicle that creates movement toward hope.

ANATOMY OF A LAMENT, USING PSALM 13 (ESV)

Complaint (questioning in misery):

> How long, O Lord ? Will you forget me forever?
> How long will you hide your face from me?
> How long must I take counsel in my soul
> and have sorrow in my heart all the day?
> How long shall my enemy be exalted over me?

Petitioning (asking the Lord to act):

> Consider and answer me, O Lord my God;
> light up my eyes, lest I sleep the sleep of death,
> lest my enemy say, "I have prevailed over him,"
> lest my foes rejoice because I am shaken.

Praise (hope/assurance in the Lord's character):

> But I have trusted in your steadfast love;
> my heart shall rejoice in your salvation.
> I will sing to the Lord,
> because he has dealt bountifully with me.

WRITING YOUR OWN LAMENT

Using the anatomy of lament as a guide, write a lament for one of the options below:

- Your city/neighborhood
- Your job/school
- Your family
- Your personal suffering

Encouragement. It can feel uncomfortable to write complaints to the Lord, and you may want to quickly hurry to the praise and resolution. I want to encourage you not to do that. The Lord invites us to cast our cares on him (1 Peter 5:7), and the invitation is good. He's not surprised by your complaints, nor is he judging you as lacking faith. He is pleased you have accepted the invitation to come. Remember to fully exhaust your complaint before moving on to the next portion of your psalm of lament. It will be a much richer experience if you do.

PRAY

Gracious Father, thank you for the invitation to cast our cares on you, knowing that you really do care for us. Thank you for being a God who weeps over your children and the brokenness and injustices of our world. Teach us how to lament in such a way that moves us toward greater hope in you with the belief that you are making all things new. In the name of our weeping Savior we pray, amen.

Bowery Mission
The Bowery Mission
The Bowery Mission
Rebuilding Lives Since 1879
bowery.org

WEEK 6
CONFRONTING THE IDOL OF COMFORT

For by the grace given me I say to every one of you:
Do not think of yourself more highly than you ought, but rather
think of yourself with sober judgment, in accordance
with the faith God has distributed to each of you.

ROMANS 12:3

GROUP SESSION INTRODUCTION

Last week we considered the Lord's lamentation for Israel's coming judgment, his invitation for them to seek him and live, and his exhortation for them to let justice roll down like a river. Our lesson this week begins with caution to those in Israel who have become complacent and overconfidently at ease, to the neglect of those around them.

> Woe to you who are complacent in Zion,
> and to you who feel secure on Mount Samaria,
> you notable men of the foremost nation,
> to whom the people of Israel come! . . .
> You lie on beds adorned with ivory
> and lounge on your couches.
> You dine on choice lambs
> and fattened calves.
> You strum away on your harps like David
> and improvise on musical instruments.
> You drink wine by the bowlful
> and use the finest lotions,
> but you do not grieve over the ruin of Joseph.
> Therefore you will be among the first to go into exile;
> your feasting and lounging will end. (Amos 6:1, 4-7)

OPENING PRAYER

Father, we admit that we have limited sight and often fail to see ourselves clearly, so we ask that you would cause us to see ourselves as you see us. Help us to receive with joy the grace necessary to look more like you everywhere we're lacking, in Jesus' name, amen. (from Romans 12:3 and 2 Corinthians 3:18)

SCRIPTURE

Read aloud Amos 6:1-14.

VIDEO

Watch this week's video.

GROUP DISCUSSION

1. What, if anything, about Chris Arnade's story in the video made you uncomfortable? Is there a particular fear or other emotion you can name? What might your response reveal about how you see God? How you see yourself?
2. Chris described himself as part of the "front row," or the mainstream, in the United States. How would you describe yourself? He described the people on the margins of society that he met as "back row" people: the working poor, the unemployed, widows, those with mental illness, drug addicts, and sex workers. Which category of persons would you be able to relate to easiest? With which category might you find it difficult to connect?
3. A change to Chris's route home put him in proximity to suffering and caused him to see with greater compassion. What small routine change might put you in closer proximity with people who have different needs than yours? How comfortable are you with that idea? Explain why.
4. Read Deuteronomy 8:11-14. In what ways do we forget the Lord? What heart condition leads to our forgetfulness? How is love of neighbor impacted when we forget the Lord?
5. What neighborhoods in your area do you think of as ruined or places you would avoid? How do you hear God's reprimand regarding Israel's lack of grief "over the ruin of Joseph" in Amos 6:6?

CLOSING PRAYER

Father, thank you for your goodness in all that you have provided for us. We forget the gospel daily and pridefully move about in your world as though we accomplished something on our own. All that we have, you have given us. Melt away every stony place in our hearts and fill us with compassion and grief for the suffering of others, amen.

DAY 1

WHAT DOES THE TEXT SAY?

With my lips I recount all the laws that come from your mouth.
I rejoice in following your statutes as one rejoices in great riches.

PSALM 119:13-14

PRAY

Lord, thank you for the opportunity to feast on your Word. Help me to rehearse these truths with my mouth and in my life, in Christ's name, amen. (from Psalm 119:13-14 and Hebrews 5:14)

READ

Amos 6:1-14

OBSERVE

1. How does verse 1 describe the mood of those in Zion (Jerusalem) and Samaria (Israel)?

2. What question does God ask Israel concerning the nations of Kalneh, Hamath, and Gath in verse 2?

3. Describe the luxurious comforts listed in verses 4-6 that Israel is enjoying. Why is this problematic, according to verse 6?

4. What does God, on oath, declare he hates in verse 8? What resulting destruction does verse 11 reveal?

5. What charges are made against Israel in verse 12?

6. To what does Israel attribute their success in verse 13?

7. In verse 14, how does the Lord promise he will respond to Israel oppressing her disadvantaged neighbors?

REFLECT

What are some ways you can incorporate remembering the gospel into your daily rhythms?

DAY 2

WHAT DOES THE TEXT MEAN? PART 1

I have hidden your word in my heart that I might not sin against you.

PSALM 119:11

PRAY

"Teach me your way, O LORD, that I may walk in your truth; unite my heart to fear your name" (Psalm 86:11 ESV).

READ

Amos 6:1-14

DEFINING OUR TERMS

What does it mean that Israel was not grieved over the ruin of Joseph (verse 6)?

> ***Grieved* (*khalah*) is to be or become weak, sick, diseased, or sorry.**

Grieved, khalah (khaw-law'), is to be or become weak, sick, diseased, or sorry.[1] Some commentators describe the "ruin of Joseph" as simply the impending disaster for Israel or the coming exile. Others suggest that because the two main tribes of Israel were Ephraim and Manasseh, the sons of Joseph, their lack of compassion and neglect for the least of those in Israel was referred to as the "ruin of Joseph."[2]

What does it mean that a nation will *oppress* Israel (v. 14)?

> **The *oppressed* or the *crushed* are those burdened with cruel or unjust impositions; it also includes the intimidation and exploitation (with overtones of extortion and violence) of weaker members of the community by those who are stronger.**

To *oppress*, or *lakhats* (law-khats'), is to crush with cruel or unjust impositions, including through violence (see 6:3) toward weaker members of the community by those who are stronger. As Israel has practiced oppressing the vulnerable, God promises to send a stronger nation who will oppress the oppressor. This promise is a restatement of the covenant curses for disobedience found in Deuteronomy 28.

AT EASE IN ZION

The opening words of chapter 6 are a warning to those who have found ease and security in what they have and where they live. Amos specifically highlights the influence of "the notable men" (ESV) that Israel seeks instead of seeking their God. He asks the question "Are you better than these kingdoms?" (ESV), calling to mind other territories larger than them that have already fallen to Assyria. Israel practices violence as though disaster could never reach their walls, so confident in the security of their wealth.

Leisure in opulent living is the image that is painted in verses 4-6. There is no pleasure too extravagant or excessive—ivory beds, bowls of wine, the most tender lamb from the flock, and the finest of oils. These luxuries came at the expense of the ruin of Joseph—the exploitation of the two main tribes of Israel, Ephraim and Manasseh.

The warning is jarring because all is well. For them, it's a beautiful day. The sun is shining, and destruction is the farthest thing from their minds. But as they have one more sip of wine and one more bite of lamb, the seeds for their destruction have been planted. Their days of leisure lounging and joyful revelry are quickly coming to an end, and Amos tells them so.

READING THE PROPHETS WELL: DIVINE OATH FORMULA

When Yahweh uses the language of swearing by himself, the phrase is called divine oath formula. In Amos 4:2, "the Lord God has sworn by his holiness" (ESV), and in this chapter, "the Lord God has sworn by himself" (Amos 6:8 ESV). The weight of the oath brings an imminent certainty.

When an oath is taken, the person taking the oath swears by something higher than himself. Because there is no one higher, God swears by his own unchanging character, or by himself. The divine oath is invoked once again in 8:7 as "The Lord has sworn by the pride of Jacob" (ESV). This seems contradictory as he has stated his abhorrence for "the pride of Jacob" in 6:8. The current and perverse pride of Jacob is their wealth and their strongholds, but the good and right pride of Jacob is their covenant God. In swearing by "the pride of Jacob" here, he is swearing by himself.[3] Other prophets record divine oaths, including Isaiah (45:23) and Jeremiah (22:5; 51:14).

EXAMINE

1. In verse 1, Amos names the seats of military strength for both Judah (Zion) and Israel (Samaria) as the places of the people's ease and security. Why was it a problem for them to feel secure in their fortresses? Describe how God feels about their fortresses in verse 8.

2. According to verse 2, how reasonable is it for Israel to think that they are secure in their actions?

3. What does verse 3 reveal about how their prideful self-sufficiency has led them to think and act?

4. What are the indicators of luxurious living in verses 4-6? Consider this opulence against the backdrop of what's happening in the land. Why is their luxurious living particularly egregious?

5. Why is it significant that verse 6 uses the word "grieve" to describe how Israel should feel about the plight of those around her? How is this different from concern or sympathy?

6. According to verse 14, what will happen to the nation that oppresses its poor? Is God just in oppressing the oppressor? Why or why not?

REFLECT

How might it look for a nation to suffer oppression? Can you think of any modern examples?

DAY 3

WHAT DOES THE TEXT MEAN? PART 2

Your statutes are my delight; they are my counselors.

PSALM 119:24

PRAY

Lord, help me to delight in your Word. May I sit in its company like that of a faithful friend, amen. (from Psalm 119:24)

READ

Amos 6:1-14

A RECKONING FOR THE IDOL OF COMFORT

Amos lists a number of actions that are indicators of Israel's self-indulgent way of life: lying on beds of ivory; eating lamb and choice calves; singing and making merriment; drinking wine; and anointing themselves with the finest of oils. He paints a vivid picture of Israel luxuriating before finally turning to say, "but you do not grieve over the ruin of Joseph." They are not grieved, deeply affected, and moved to action by the plight of others. Comfort has clearly become their idol. The "therefore" in verse 7 indicates Yahweh's intolerance of the god of comfort and moves our focus to the grave consequence Israel will experience as a result of her illicit worship. Those named would be the first ones to go into exile and their celebrating would indeed cease.

Once again, Amos uses the word *justice* (*mishpat*) and its closely linked counterpart *tsedaqah*, the word for righteousness or being just, to highlight Israel's injustices. Verse 12 uses rhetorical questions, as we also saw done in Amos 3:3-6, to highlight the absurdity of injustice. It is not the expected order of things any more than horses running on rocks or plowing rocks with oxen (Amos 6:12). Injustice among Yahweh's covenant people is just as blatant of a break to the natural order. Breaks in the prescribed, covenantal order bring the expected, righteous judgment of Yahweh. He promises that as Israel has oppressed others without turning back to him, he will now oppress them from the Lebo-hamath (the northern boundary of Israel) to the Brook of the Arabah (the southern boundary of Judah). His justice will permeate the entirety of the northern and southern kingdoms.

Today we know that the fullness of God's judgment on Israel and Judah was a mere pointer to the fullness of the justice that would be laid upon Christ on behalf of the believer. Much more than for only Israel and Judah, Yahweh is the God who practices justice in all the earth (Jeremiah 9:24). Those who are in union with Christ are both called and empowered to participate in this work of practicing justice by being gripped again and again by the gospel of grace, which loosens us from the hold of the idol of comfort.

EXAMINE

1. We've discussed the marks of self-indulgent excess represented in Amos 6:4-6. What follows the word "but" in verse 6 that announces the presenting issue with Israel being preoccupied with their own comfort?

2. Verse 7 predicts a time when Israel's revelry (festive noise) would pass away. What festive sounds do verses 4-6 invite us to hear? What sounds would you expect to hear as the people are being carried away into exile?

3. What idols of comfort does the Lord go after in verse 11?

4. Verse 12 describes justice in the life of the believer as the natural order of things. What injustice do you find absurd? Explain why.

5. How does the Lord raising up a nation to discipline Israel inform how you think about both good and wicked rulers?

6. Why is it good news that God's full and complete judgment was laid on Jesus? Describe how believers are both complicit in Christ's death and beneficiaries of its rewards.

REFLECT

How should our participation in the greatest injustice of all time, the death of Christ, inform how we approach injustice?

DAY 4

WHAT DOES THE REST OF SCRIPTURE SAY?

Blessed is the one who does not walk in step with the wicked or stand in the way that sinners take or sit in the company of mockers, but whose delight is in the law of the LORD, and who meditates on his law day and night.

PSALM 1:1-2

PRAY

"Make me understand the way of your precepts, and I will meditate on your wondrous works" (Psalm 119:27 ESV).

READ

Amos 6:1-14

SEARCH THE SCRIPTURES

1. Consider these Scripture examples of the divine oath formula. Who or what is God swearing by? What is he promising to bring to pass?

The Lord GOD has sworn by his holiness that, behold, the days are coming upon you, when they shall take you away with hooks, even the last of you with fishhooks. **(Amos 4:2 ESV)**	*By myself I have sworn; from my mouth has gone out in righteousness a word that shall not return: "To me every knee shall bow, every tongue shall swear allegiance."* **(Isaiah 45:23 ESV)**	*But if you will not obey these words, I swear by myself, declares the LORD, that this house shall become a desolation.* **(Jeremiah 22:5 ESV)**	*The LORD of hosts has sworn by himself: Surely I will fill you with men, as many as locusts, and they shall raise the shout of victory over you.* **(Jeremiah 51:14 ESV)**

2. Who is being called out in Amos 6:1? How is this different from in 4:1? How is it the same?

3. Those lying on beds of ivory in verse 4 were not lying down to sleep, but reclining at feasts.[4] The value of their goods is not what's being called into question, however, but the great cost and cruelty it cost their neighbors. Consider the opulence of ivory in the ancient world by examining the following verses. Is the context in which ivory is used here similar or different from in 6:4? Explain why.

The king also made a great ivory throne and overlaid it with the finest gold. **(1 Kings 10:18 ESV)**	*For the king had a fleet of ships of Tarshish at sea with the fleet of Hiram. Once every three years the fleet of ships of Tarshish used to come bringing gold, silver, ivory, apes, and peacocks.* **(1 Kings 10:22 ESV)**	*Your robes are all fragrant with myrrh and aloes and cassia. From ivory palaces stringed instruments make you glad.* **(Psalm 45:8 ESV)**	*Now the rest of the acts of Ahab and all that he did, and the ivory house that he built and all the cities that he built, are they not written in the Book of the Chronicles of the Kings of Israel?* **(1 Kings 22:39 ESV)**

4. In verse 8, God's hatred exposes a righteous judgment against wickedness, namely the pride of Jacob. Consider these other verses and discuss what it is that the Lord hates and what it says about what he values.

I hate, I despise your feasts, and I take no delight in your solemn assemblies. **(Amos 5:21 ESV)**	*There are six things that the LORD hates, seven that are detestable to him: haughty eyes, a lying tongue, hands that shed innocent blood, a heart that devises wicked schemes, feet that are quick to rush into evil, a false witness who pours out lies and a person who stirs up conflict in the community.* **(Proverbs 6:16-19)**	*The Sovereign LORD has sworn by himself—the LORD God Almighty declares: "I abhor the pride of Jacob and detest his fortresses; I will deliver up the city and everything in it."* **(Amos 6:8)**

REFLECT

Which of God's values did you most need to be reminded of today? How are you challenged by this value?

DAY 5

PRACTICING JUSTICE

Blessed is he whose help is the God of Jacob, whose hope is in the Lord his God, . . . who executes justice for the oppressed, who gives food to the hungry.

PSALM 146:5,7 (ESV)

PRAY

Father, teach us now how to participate in the work that you are doing in your world by being agents of justice for the oppressed and being generous to those in need, in Jesus' name, amen. (from Psalm 146:7)

READ

Amos 6:1-14

RESPOND

1. You may remember from week 1 that the idol of comfort presents as an excessive desire for avoidance of pain or stress and is evidenced as seeking freedom from responsibilities, expectations, or anything that might feel unpleasant. What discomfort are you most likely to seek to avoid? How has that looked in your life?

2. In what do you feel the greatest security? How might that security be the enemy of dependence and compassion?

3. How do you distinguish between good self-care and over-indulgence in your own life?

4. How might a hyper focus on your own comfort dull your concern for the evil around you?

5. As part of the songbook of Israel, Psalm 103 was a reminder to remember the benefits of being God's children and how he longs to satisfy us. Read the psalm below. Discuss the places in your life where you are experiencing contentment.

Praise the Lord, my soul;
 all my inmost being, praise his holy name.
Praise the Lord, my soul,
 and forget not all his benefits . . .
who satisfies your desires with good things
 so that your youth is renewed like the eagle's.
The Lord works righteousness
 and justice for all the oppressed. (Psalm 103:1-2, 5-6)

6. Discuss the places in your life where you are feeling discontented and need to remember the Lord's benefits. How might rehearsing these truths lead you to greater contentment, even in adversity? How might "being grieved over the ruin of Joseph," or having a focus on someone else's need, lead to greater contentment?

PRAY

Lord, we are so grateful that you have promised to be our help. We have been socialized in a culture of inequity that has dulled our awareness of evil and the plight of the oppressed. Give us eyes that see clearly and hearts that beat in the direction of your ways. Give us hearts that are deeply grieved by the sin, wickedness, and hurt all around us. Give us the courage to call out injustice and the wisdom to participate in the restoration of people and the rebuilding of devastated places for your glory, amen.

WEEK 7
COMPASSION: THE COMPANION TO JUSTICE

Therefore, I tell you, her many sins have been forgiven—as her great love has shown. But whoever has been forgiven little loves little.

LUKE 7:47

GROUP SESSION INTRODUCTION

In our previous session, we looked at the message of caution to the complacent and overconfidently at ease in Israel, and we considered how an excessive desire for comfort can lead to the neglect of those around us. This lesson examines the five visions the Lord showed Amos concerning Israel, and we learn that Amos is not just a bearer of hard news, but a tender intercessor who pleads for God's mercy.

> This is what he showed me: The Lord was standing by a wall that had been built true to plumb, with a plumb line in his hand. And the LORD asked me, "What do you see, Amos?"
>
> "A plumb line," I replied.
>
> Then the Lord said, "Look, I am setting a plumb line among my people Israel; I will spare them no longer." (Amos 7:7-8)

OPENING PRAYER

Father, as we continue to consider your righteous judgment against sin, would you deepen our understanding of how much greater and deeper your grace reaches? Increase our awareness of your grace working in every aspect of our lives, and make us those who are quick to be conduits of that same grace to others—in Christ's name, amen. (from Romans 5:20-21 and Luke 7:47)

SCRIPTURE

Read aloud Amos 7:1–8:14.

VIDEO

Watch this week's video.

GROUP DISCUSSION

1. Describe your experience of wrestling with the weightiness of Israel's judgments as we've studied the book of Amos. Chapter nine of Amos contains good news; how does it now feel to anticipate that "Sunday's coming"? What would you have missed if the study focused only on the good news at the end?
2. A couple of the verses of poetry in chapter eight bear great resemblance to the Gospel of Mark's description of Jesus' crucifixion (such as Mark 15:33). Some people would describe the tension of Good Friday as both celebratory and somber. Discuss why that might be. Why might studying prophetic judgment bear a similar tension?
3. The Gospels repeatedly mention that Jesus was "moved by compassion" (Matthew 9:36, 14:14; Luke 7:13). How does considering Jesus' compassion toward the suffering help you think about your relationship to the suffering of others?
4. Luke 7 introduces a sinful woman who had an awareness of her great need for God's grace. How might growing in awareness of our own sinfulness aid our love for others? How can we grow in this way?
5. What truth have you seen most consistently concerning God's heart in judgment?
6. What form of human suffering most quickly moves you to show compassion, and for what people group(s) in particular? Discuss the heart attitude that moves you to such compassion.
7. What form of human suffering are you least likely to have compassion for? Consider the people group(s) most affected. Discuss the heart attitude that hinders such compassion.

CLOSING PRAYER

Lord, cause us to be so gripped by the gospel of grace that we would be those who love much, amen.

DAY 1

WHAT DOES THE TEXT SAY?

Your word is a lamp for my feet, a light on my path.

PSALM 119:105

PRAY

Lord, teach me your Word that I might be guided by truth in all my ways, in Christ's name, amen.

READ

Amos 7:1–8:14

THE FIRST FOUR VISIONS

Amos is moved to compassionate, fervent prayer in response to three visions the Lord shows him concerning Israel. In the first vision, Amos is shown locusts consuming Israel's crops. This imagery would have harkened back to the plague of locusts the Lord sent while Israel was being oppressed by Pharaoh in Egypt (Exodus 10:13-15). Each plague was a targeted attack on Egypt's gods. Now for Israel, their crops, a significant source of income in their agrarian society, were being threatened. Amos's cry gives us a sense of the seriousness of such a judgment: "Sovereign Lord, forgive! How can Jacob survive? He is so small!" (Amos 7:2). Amos pleads for the Lord's mercies toward Israel, and the Lord relents.

In the second vision, Amos is shown judgment by fire that covers the land and sea. Again Amos cries out to the Lord, "Sovereign Lord, I beg you, stop! How can Jacob survive? He is so small!" (Amos 7:5). Amos's cry magnifies the enormity of this great God and the helplessness of Israel in response to his judgments. Amos again begs for the Lord's mercies, and the Lord relents.

In the third vision, Amos is shown the Lord standing beside a wall with a plumb line, or a measuring device, in his hand. Plumb lines serve as a standard for verifying that a wall is level or confirming that it needs to be torn down because it isn't level. Metaphorically the plumb line represents the righteous standard to which Israel had failed to adhere, and they would now be removed from their land like an unlevel wall. The Lord says, "I will never again pass by them" (Amos 7:8 ESV)—in other words, he will not relent from his judgment—and alerts Amos that any further intercession is futile.

In his great mercy, the Lord delays executing his justice in the first two visions, allowing his people the opportunity to turn to him in repentance. The third vision reminds us that he won't withhold his judgment forever. The apostle Peter would state this idea later in 2 Peter 3:9: "The Lord is not slow in keeping his promise, as some understand slowness. Instead he is patient with you, not wanting anyone to perish, but everyone to come to repentance."

In the fourth vision, Amos sees a basket of summer fruit, again signaling that the end has come and the Lord will no longer "pass them by," or withhold his judgment. Amos speaks both charges against Israel and a foreshadowing of the Messiah through prophetic poetry. This is consistent with how we've seen the severest of judgments be interlaced with a depth of compassion.

OBSERVE

1. In chapter seven, what phrase is repeated in verses 1, 4, and 7 that indicates prophetic vision?

2. What concern does Amaziah the priest bring to King Jeroboam concerning Amos in 7:10-11?

3. What are the first words we hear Amaziah the priest speak to Amos in 7:12-13?

4. How does Amos describe his calling in verses 14 and 15? What was his occupation before becoming a prophet?

5. What startling prophecy does Amos give concerning Amaziah and Israel in verse 17?

6. What does 8:2 say is the meaning of the vision of the summer fruit?

7. Amos 8:4-12 is an extensive poem describing Israel's final judgment. Read verses 9-10 and describe the particularly dark day that's coming.

REFLECT

Have you ever been so moved by someone else's difficulty that you cried out to God about it? If so, describe the situation.

DAY 2

WHAT DOES THE TEXT MEAN? PART 1

The unfolding of your words gives light;
it gives understanding to the simple.

PSALM 119:130

PRAY

Lord, please bring clarity and understanding as I study your Word, amen. (from Psalm 119:130)

READ

Amos 7:1–8:14

DEFINING OUR TERMS

What does it mean that the Lord *relented*?

> ***Relented* (*nakham*) is to be moved to pity, to have compassion.**

In response to the visions the Lord shows Amos, concerning the coming judgment suffering of Israel, Amos cries out to God for mercy. In response to Amos's cries for Israel, the Lord relented. *Relented, nakham* (naw-kham'), means to be moved to pity, to have compassion.[1]

Unlike other prophets, Noah for instance, who wanted to see those to whom he prophesied be punished, Amos did not. Amos longed for God to be merciful to Israel. His posture of mercy reflected God's heart for the people—longsuffering, merciful, and patient with Israel in their unfaithfulness.

What is the purpose of sackcloth?

> ***Sackcloth* (*saq*) was worn in mourning and humiliation, either as a loose garment like a sack, or a piece of similar material; it could also be the same garment spread out to lie on.**

Sackcloth, *saq* (saq), was worn in mourning and humiliation, either as a loose garment like a sack, or a piece of similar material (of rough, dark hair), fastened around the body. It could also be the same garment or material spread out to lie on. Similarly, shaving the head was also a sign that expressed mourning.

READING THE PROPHETS WELL: PROPHETIC VISION AND THE SEER

In verse 12, Amaziah the priest addresses the prophet Amos as "seer." Seer was a designation given to prophets whom the Lord spoke to through visual prophecy. Amos affirms seeing messages from the Lord in the opening verse of the book and again in his five visionary experiences: Amos 7:1-3, 4-6, 7-9; 8:1-3; 9:1-4.

Other prophets evidence being seers, as both Isaiah and Jeremiah received their calls in visions (Isaiah 6 and Jeremiah 1). Also, Ezekiel (Ezekiel 1; 4:37; 8:11; 40–48), Daniel (Daniel 7–12), and Zechariah (Zechariah 1:7–6:15) further establish the popularity of the visionary form in the Babylonian and Persian periods.[2]

THE FIVE VISIONS

Complete the chart for four of the five visions described in Amos 7:1–8:14. The first one is done for you.

REFLECT

How would you pray if you believed that your cry to the Lord changed what happens in the earth? Can you imagine that God would ever relent, or turn from his action, because you asked?

The five visions

What Amos Saw "The Sovereign LORD showed me . . ."	*Meaning*	*Responses* Who responded? What they said	*Compassion* Who shows compassion? How?
Forming locusts (Amos 7:1-2)	Locusts would destroy their crops.	Amos begged the Lord to forgive Israel. The Lord relented.	Amos interceded with compassion. The Lord withheld judgment.
Judgment by fire (Amos 7:4)	Israel would be destroyed by fire.		
The plumb line (Amos 7:7-9)	The Lord judged Israel by a righteous standard, and they were found unfaithful to the covenant.		
Summer fruit (Amos 8:1-3)	It was the end of Israel's season of God's patience; it had ended, and they were ripe for judgment.	Amos speaks the words of the Lord in poetry describing the charges against them and the severity of their coming judgment.	The Lord gives prophetic poetry foreshadowing the death of Christ, the ultimate fulfillment of judgment.
The Lord standing beside the altar (Amos 9:1-4)	Inescapable judgment was coming to Israel as they go into captivity at the hands of their enemies.		"'I will not utterly destroy the house of Jacob,' declares the LORD." Amos 9:8 (ESV)

DAY 3

WHAT DOES THE TEXT MEAN? PART 2

But the Advocate, the Holy Spirit, whom the Father will send in my name, will teach you all things and will remind you of everything I have said to you.

JOHN 14:26

PRAY

Father, teach me now by your Spirit. Help me to recall the truths I am learning and apply them in my living, in Christ's name, amen. (from John 14:26)

READ

Amos 7:1–8:14

THE HOUSE OF JEROBOAM RESPONDS

In verse 10, we finally get to see how Amos's words are being received. Amaziah, the priest of Bethel, has sent news of Amos's prophecies to King Jeroboam, including notice that King Jeroboam would die by the sword and Israel would be taken into exile. Amaziah addresses Amos directly, calling him "seer" (7:12) or *prophet*, acknowledging the validity of his work but commanding him to never again prophecy at Bethel because it "is the king's sanctuary" (7:13). Amaziah's statements highlight the reality of worship at Bethel. It is not the authorized place of worship that's in the southern kingdom, erected for the one true God, Yahweh. Instead, this place was erected as Jeroboam's sanctuary, deceiving those who would seek to worship Yahweh. The text doesn't suggest that Amaziah didn't believe Amos was telling the truth. That wasn't the central issue for him. Amos's words threatened Jeroboam's power over the people of Israel, the sole reason he sanctioned worship in this northern temple (1 Kings 12:25-30). Amos's words challenged his power structures and idols of power and control, causing him to seek to silence Amos by asking him to leave.

In the final verses of the chapter, Amos responds to Amaziah's command to stop prophesying and to leave Israel. Here we learn the details of his call—his occupation before coming to Israel and the Lord's command for him to go prophesy to Israel. Amos makes it clear that the message he's giving to them was not his idea, and that seeking to silence his voice would come at great cost to Amaziah the priest, his family, the land, and all of Israel.

Amos left his home in Judah to identify with the citizens of Israel. He spoke truth to them and with a heart of compassion cried out to the God of the universe on their behalf. Amos paints a vivid picture for us of a Christ who left the riches of heaven to become poor and identify with a people who would reject him. He spoke truth urging all people to repent, to turn to the God who loves them. And having taken on the punishment we justly deserve, Jesus is now seated at the right hand of the Father and lives to make compassionate intercession for us. We learn from both Amos and Jesus that justice requires being proximate to the plight of others. It involves the surrender of our rights, comfort, and benefits so that others might gain the same. It involves a surrender of our freedoms so that others can be made free.

EXAMINE

1. Why might a vision concerning summer fruit be particularly effective to a "dresser of sycamore figs" (Amos 7:14 ESV)? How might such language be helpful in an agrarian society?

2. Read the charges against Israel in Amos 2:6-7. Compare it with the charges in Amos 8:4-6. How are they the same? How are they different?

3. Why is it significant that the famine Israel would experience would be a famine for something they couldn't buy (see Amos 8:11)?

POETIC FORESHADOWING OF CHRIST

As we have developed our interpretive grid for reading the Prophets well, we have engaged with various literary devices found in the book of Amos. We started the book looking at oracles of judgment on surrounding nations and Israel (Amos 1–2). We have seen rhetorical questions indicating the natural order of events and the certainty of judgment following unrepentant, willful disobedience (Amos 3). We looked at direct speech between the prophet Amos and Amaziah the priest (Amos 7). We considered beautiful poetry of the God of creation describing himself (Amos 5). Verse 4 of chapter eight is also poetry—not the beautiful language of God's majesty in creation, but charges against Israel put to poetic verse.

The themes captured in this poetry are not new but very familiar: mistreatment of the poor, deceitful business practices, and ill-gotten gain. While we may hear these themes as just a repeat of what's been said before, they underline the incredible grace, patience, and care the Lord is expressing in allowing space for Israel to repent. Even before the time of Amos's message, the Lord sent other prophets to call Israel back to the heart of God (Amos 2:11). The repetition magnifies the sheer amount of grace and patience the Lord has poured out on his people. He's been incredibly kind to them. In all of the repetition and repeated themes we get just a small sense of how longsuffering the Lord has been with Israel, and with us.

As the Lord continues to declare judgment in poetic verse, he alludes to a day when the judgment of the world would be laid upon his Son. He says in Amos 8:9, "I will make the sun go down at noon and darken the earth in broad daylight." The prophet Joel similarly anticipates the day when the cosmos would be darkened. Mark 15:33 reveals that darkness covered the whole land from the sixth until the ninth hour when Jesus was being crucified for the sins of the world he created. Amos describes the horrors of this day as "like mourning for an only son and the end of it like a bitter day" (Amos 8:10). As God is pronouncing judgment on Israel, glimmers of hope emerge as he points to his only Son and the bitterest of days. He points to the day when Jesus would ultimately take on the punishment the nations deserve and in exchange offer the righteousness they could never attain on their own merit. Amid certain judgment is deep mercy, a coming remedy in Christ Jesus.

EXAMINE

1. What does King Jeroboam and Amaziah the priest seek to protect? How were Amos's words a threat to what they valued?

2. What two things did Amaziah command Amos to do or stop doing? How does his command demonstrate the specific offense Jesus charged against Israel in Amos 2:12?

3. What did Amaziah call Amos that suggests he believed Amos's words were truly from God? What does Amaziah demonstrate about the relationship between knowing and practicing truth?

4. In Amos 7:14-15, Amos shares his calling narrative with Amaziah. Why might it have been important to share this story at this point? Who was Amaziah speaking on behalf of? Who was Amos speaking on behalf of?

5. What do we learn about Amos's compulsion to speak truth based on his answer to Amaziah?

REFLECT

Is there a calling that you're so convinced of that no one can talk you out of it? If so, what is it?

DAY 4

WHAT DOES THE REST OF SCRIPTURE SAY?

All Scripture is God-breathed and is useful for teaching, rebuking, correcting and training in righteousness, so that the servant of God may be thoroughly equipped for every good work.

2 TIMOTHY 3:16-17

PRAY

Lord Jesus, would you build me up with the truth of your Word that I might do the good work of living justly before you, in Christ's name, amen. (from 2 Timothy 3:16-17)

READ

Amos 7:1–8:14

SEARCH THE SCRIPTURES

1. Consider the severity of the plague of locusts on Egypt in Exodus 10:1-15. Read Deuteronomy 7:7 and consider Israel's size compared to the surrounding nations. Why might Amos's plea for Israel following the first vision (Amos 7:2-3) have been so urgent?

2. We see from Amos 1:1, 7:12, and 7:15 that Amos was from the southern kingdom of Judah but had come to Israel out of the calling to prophesy. How do you think his proximity to Israel affected his concern for them?

3. Read these examples of the Lord relenting from disaster. Consider in each example what causes him to relent. What does each scenario reveal about the Lord's purpose in judgment?

So the LORD sent a pestilence on Israel from the morning until the appointed time. . . . And when the angel stretched out his hand toward Jerusalem to destroy it, the LORD relented from the calamity and said to the angel who was working destruction among the people, "It is enough; now stay your hand." . . . So the LORD responded to the plea for the land, and the plague was averted from Israel. **(2 Samuel 24:15-16, 25 ESV)**	*And the LORD said to Moses, "I have seen this people, and behold, it is a stiff-necked people. Now therefore let me alone, that my wrath may burn hot against them. . . ." But Moses implored the LORD his God and said, . . . "Turn from your burning anger and relent from this disaster against your people. Remember Abraham, Isaac, and Israel, your servants, to whom you swore by your own self, and said to them, 'I will multiply your offspring as the stars of heaven.'" . . . And the LORD relented from the disaster that he had spoken of bringing on his people.* **(Exodus 32:9-14 ESV)**	*Jonah began to go into the city, going a day's journey. And he called out, "Yet forty days, and Nineveh shall be overthrown!" And the people of Nineveh believed God. They called for a fast and put on sackcloth, from the greatest of them to the least of them. . . . When God saw what they did, how they turned from their evil way, God relented of the disaster that he had said he would do to them, and he did not do it.* **(Jonah 3:4-5, 10 ESV)**	*If at any time I declare concerning a nation or a kingdom, that I will pluck up and break down and destroy it, and if that nation, concerning which I have spoken, turns from its evil, I will relent of the disaster that I intended to do to it.* **(Jeremiah 18:7-8 ESV)**

4. Use the following verses to discuss what the "plumb line," or standard for righteous living, is for the believer in Christ.

One thing I do: forgetting what lies behind and straining forward to what lies ahead, I press on toward the goal for the prize of the upward call of God in Christ Jesus. **(Philippians 3:13-14 ESV)**	*Do not conform to the pattern of this world, but be transformed by the renewing of your mind. Then you will be able to test and approve what God's will is—his good, pleasing and perfect will.* **(Romans 12:2)**	*Have the same mindset as Christ Jesus.* **(Philippians 2:5)**	*Love one another. As I have loved you, so you must love one another.* **(John 13:34)**

5. In the Scriptures, false balances are a symbol of injustice through dishonest gain. Consider the passages below. What does the Lord value in the law he's given? How does he regard rebellion against this law?

You shall do no wrong in judgment, in measures of length or weight or quantity. You shall have just balances, just weights, a just ephah, and a just hin: I am the Lord your God, who brought you out of the land of Egypt. **(Leviticus 19:35-36 ESV)**	*Unequal weights and unequal measures are both alike an abomination to the Lord.* **(Proverbs 20:10 ESV)**	*Can I forget any longer the treasures of wickedness in the house of the wicked, and the scant measure that is accursed? Shall I acquit the man with wicked scales and with a bag of deceitful weights?* **(Micah 6:10-11 ESV)**

6. Compare and contrast the poem of lament in Amos 8:9-10 with Mark 15:33-41. What's the same about these passages? What's different?

7. In Amos 8:9-10 the Lord alludes to a bitter day when judgment would fall on his only Son. During the rebellion of our first parents as recorded in Genesis 3, the Father alludes to hope amid judgment. Genesis 3:15 is often called the first preaching of the gospel, and it is preached by the Father himself. Read Genesis 3:14-15; how is it similar to Amos 8:9-10? How is it different? What is consistent about the character of God in each?

REFLECT

What do you know that the Lord values from the Scripture verses you read today?

DAY 5

PRACTICING JUSTICE

Jesus replied, "Anyone who loves me will obey my teaching. My Father will love them, and we will come to them and make our home with them."

JOHN 14:23

PRAY

Father, please help my love for you to be proven genuine in how I walk in your ways of love for others, in Christ's name, amen. (from John 13:34 and 14:23)

READ

Amos 7:1–8:14

RESPOND

1. Do you really believe that the Lord stops or starts activity in the earth in response to your prayers? Discuss why or why not.

2. How might the places where you live, work, and play look different if you focused on them with compassionate prayer? How might such prayer shape your desire for doing justice?

3. Discuss a time when you've met opposition for doing what was right. Can you think of a time when you were silenced by the rules of an organization when you felt the need to speak up? Have you ever silenced another with your actions or words?

4. The idol of control expresses itself as an excessive desire for significance achieved through success, winning, and influence. It desires to control outcomes and is often accompanied by fear. Read 1 Kings 12:25-30. What did Jeroboam fear when he made Bethel a place of false worship? What did he fear when he sought to silence Amos?

5. What outcome in your own life do you most fear? Discuss what you might be tempted to control as a result.

6. Can you think of systems that benefit the wealthy and disadvantage the poor? Consider your work, community, city, and nation. What small step might you take to push against such a system?

7. What gospel hope do you derive from considering the bitter day of Jesus' crucifixion? How does it speak to your bitter days?

8. As the charges of unjust practices are pronounced on Israel, why does it matter that God alludes to the day his Son would suffer the greatest injustice in history? What does it say about how God values justice?

9. Do you think of yourself as a participant in the greatest injustice, the "bitter day" when Christ died for the sins of humanity? How might considering your place in the story shape how you approach injustices around you?

PRAYER

Father, I am often angry about the injustices all around me but less upset by my own role in them. Please open my eyes to my own indifference, complacency, and lack of compassion and give me specific ways to take steps toward righting the wrongs around me, amen.

WEEK 8

RESTORING PEOPLE AND REBUILDING PLACES

The Lord your God is with you,
the Mighty Warrior who saves.
He will take great delight in you;
in his love he will no longer rebuke you,
but will rejoice over you with singing.

ZEPHANIAH 3:17

GROUP SESSION INTRODUCTION

In our lesson last week, we considered four of Amos's five final visions: the locusts, fire, the plumb line, and the basket of summer fruit. This week we consider the fifth vision of the Lord standing beside the altar. We will conclude the final judgment and look to a day when all things will be made new.

"The days are coming," declares the Lord,

"when the reaper will be overtaken by the plowman
and the planter by the one treading grapes.
New wine will drip from the mountains
and flow from all the hills,
and I will bring my people Israel back from exile.
They will rebuild the ruined cities and live in them.
They will plant vineyards and drink their wine;
they will make gardens and eat their fruit.
I will plant Israel in their own land,
never again to be uprooted
from the land I have given them,"
says the Lord your God. (Amos 9:13-15)

OPENING PRAYER

Father, thank you for being in our midst when we gather to study your Word. Thank you that your heart posture toward those in covenant with you is delightful rejoicing that bursts out into loud song. How you love us! Give us hearts that respond in rejoicing and praise you for who you are, in Jesus' name, amen. (from Zephaniah 3:17 and Amos 9:5-10)

SCRIPTURE

Read aloud Amos 9:1-15.

VIDEO

Watch the introductory video.

GROUP DISCUSSION

1. We see the inescapable nature of God's presence in verses 2-4. When might this be a comfort to you? When might it feel threatening?
2. Consider the hymn of doxology (verses 5-6). What comes immediately before it? What follows it? What in those verses is worthy of praise?
3. How does a God who sings align with how you think about God? How is this similar to or different from the way you typically think about him?
4. Consider all the different literary devices we have explored in the book of Amos, including poetry, prose, rhetorical questions, direct speech, and now doxology. Why do you think the Lord opted to deliver his Word to us in so many genres and styles? Do you find that difficult or encouraging?
5. Have you ever received mercy amid discipline? How did it cause you to think about the one issuing the discipline?
6. What have you gained by spending time wading through the judgments of God given by Amos? What would you have lost by going straight to the restoration story?
7. Why might it be harmful to "heal someone's wounds lightly," or run straight to gospel good news without understanding the depth of their suffering? When might you be tempted to do this?
8. What is one thing that you must do differently as a result of this study?

CLOSING PRAYER

Father, as we begin this final week of this study, would you seal these truths to our hearts in such a way that genuine transformation springs forth, moving our feet in the paths of justice, restoration, and righteousness, amen.

DAY 1

WHAT DOES THE TEXT SAY?

Heaven and earth will pass away,
but my words will never pass away.

MATTHEW 24:35

PRAY

Father, thank you that your words are true and faithful, powerful and eternal. Help me to treasure your words as the precious, life-giving source they are, in Christ's name, amen. (from Hebrews 1:3 and Matthew 24:35)

READ

Amos 9:1-15

OBSERVE

1. How does God describe his own majesty in verses 5-6?

2. How does God mercifully limit his destruction in verse 8?

3. What words signaling restoration do you see in verses 11, 14, and 15?

4. What are all the actions God promises "I will" do in verses 11-15?

REFLECT

Has there ever been a time when the promise of God's presence was a comfort for you? Has there ever been a time when you felt threatened by God's presence? Please describe.

DAY 2

WHAT DOES THE TEXT MEAN? PART 1

They will rebuild the ancient ruins and restore the places long devastated; they will renew the ruined cities that have been devastated for generations.

ISAIAH 61:4

PRAY

Lord, according to your Word, it's the Spirit of the Lord who empowers me to be one who rebuilds and restores. Would you teach me now how to become an agent of restoration in every way your Spirit is willing to empower me, amen. (from Isaiah 61:1-4)

READ

Amos 9:1-15

DEFINING OUR TERMS

What does it mean to *repair*?

> ***Repair* (*gadar*) is to enclose what's been broken down.**

Repair (its breaches[1]), *gadar* (gaw-dar'), is to wall in or around; it's to close up, fence up, hedge, enclose what's been broken down.

What does it mean to *raise up*?

> ***Raise up* (*qum*) is to give what has been demolished what it needs to arise or stand.**

Raise up (its ruins), *qum* (koom), is to cause to arise or stand. The tense of this verb makes it reflexive, meaning to cause oneself to do something. The notion of "raising up ruins" suggests giving what has been demolished what it needs to arise or stand.

REFLECT

Consider the difference in *raising up* and *repairing*. Why are both necessary?

READING THE PROPHETS WELL: COMING RESTORATION OF ALL THINGS

The last five verses of Amos offer a beautiful picture of the restoration of Israel. In pointing us to the coming restoration, the prophets often use garden language harkening a return to the beautiful flourishing and abundance in the Garden of Eden before humanity's rebellion (Genesis 3). In Amos 9:14, Israel's participation in the restoration involves their making a garden and eating its fruit, but it's the Father himself who promises to plant them on their land where they will never again be uprooted (Amos 9:15). In doing so, he ensures that they will flourish forever in the land he gives them.

The raising up of "the booth of David" (ESV) mentioned in verse 11 points to the restoration of David's dynasty through the greater King David, Jesus Christ. The prophet Jeremiah gives us further insight, saying: "Behold, the days are coming, declares the Lord, when I will raise up for David a righteous Branch, and he shall reign as king and deal wisely, and shall execute justice and righteousness in the land" (Jeremiah 23:5 ESV). Acts 2:29-36 affirms that Jesus is the fulfillment of the promised restoration of the house of David.

Amos 9:12 points to a day when Gentiles, or "all the nations who are called by my name" (ESV), are also treated as God's own possession. The apostle James quotes the Amos 9:11-12 prophecy in Jerusalem at the first church council recorded in Acts 15:16-17. He asserts that Amos's prophecy was fulfilled in the preaching of the gospel of Jesus Christ to the Gentiles and their inclusion as the people of God in the church of Jesus Christ. Praise God that the coming restoration not only includes Israel, but Christ's church—the spiritual Israel.

Until Amos 9:11, "that day" has anticipated the day of the Lord's judgment, but now anticipates the day he will restore Israel. He promises to raise up the fallen booth of David, to restore the Davidic monarchy. The language of restoring and rebuilding found in verses 11-15 is not unique to Amos. The book of Isaiah is rich in restoration, repair, and rebuilding language. In Isaiah 58, there is an inextricable tie made to fasting and prayer and doing the work of rebuilding, repairing, and restoring. Isaiah 61 goes on to express the power by which such work is to be done:

> "The Spirit of the Lord God is upon me,
> because the Lord has anointed me to bring good news to the poor;
> he has sent me to bind up the brokenhearted. . . .
> They shall build up the ancient ruins;
> they shall raise up the former devastations;
> they shall repair the ruined cities, the devastations of many generations." (Isaiah 61:1, 4 ESV)

Nearly eight hundred years later, Jesus of Nazareth would stand and read Isaiah's words in the temple followed by the statement "Today this scripture is fulfilled in your hearing" (Luke 4:21). He indeed is the One who inaugurated a kingdom that would repair, rebuild, raise up, and restore by the Spirit of the Lord. It's the very same Spirit who has come to rest upon his church to empower her to participate in the shared kingdom work of repairing, rebuilding, raising up, and restoring.

DAY 3

WHAT DOES THE TEXT MEAN? PART 2

He who was seated on the throne said,
"I am making everything new!" Then he said,
"Write this down, for these words are trustworthy and true."

REVELATION 21:5

PRAY

Father, as I long for the day Jesus makes all things new, help me to participate in the work you are doing today, practicing steadfast love and justice, rebuilding, repairing, and restoring, amen. (from Isaiah 61:1-4 and Jeremiah 9:24)

READ

Amos 9:1-15

RESTORATION "IN THAT DAY"

Amos 9:13-15 points to "that day" when that kingdom will be fully realized and the Greater David—Jesus Christ—will return to reign and rule over all the earth. He points to a day of restoration and flourishing, plentiful harvests and joyful celebrations signified by the abundance of wine. His rule will be a righteous one, radically free from the stain of evil, full of flourishing, a kingdom in which all things are made new—a coming reality worthy of praise.

EXAMINE

1. Read 9:1-4 and complete the chart of the five visions, including the row for the fifth vision. What hope is given in how God responds?

2. Verse 12 mentions "all the nations who are called by my name" (ESV), indicating that not only is Israel the Lord's, but all the Gentile (non-Jewish) nations of the world as well. The early church references this teaching in Acts 15 to preclude Gentile believers from having to assimilate to Jewish culture and be circumcised for salvation. How does this help us understand God's relationship with Israel and his plan for Gentile nations?

3. What about the age to come described in verses 13-15 appeals to you most? How might Israel have heard it?

4. Listen to the powerful statements the Lord makes about what he will do for Israel in verses 11-15: "I will raise up . . . repair . . . rebuild . . . restore . . . plant them" (ESV). Which of these would you be most excited to hear that the Lord is doing? In which would you most want to participate?

5. Scripture uses garden language to signal a return to an ideal. The abundant crops mentioned are such a picture of flourishing. In what area do you strain to imagine how restoration could look? What makes it difficult to imagine?

REFLECT

Where do you see the Lord doing the work of raising up, repairing, rebuilding, restoring, or planting in your life? Where do you long to see this work?

DAY 4

WHAT DOES THE REST OF SCRIPTURE SAY?

Your word, Lord, is eternal; it stands firm in the heavens.

PSALM 119:89

PRAY

Lord, thank you that your truth is firmly fixed and unchanging. I can rely on it to guide me in the way that pleases you and that leads to flourishing, amen. (from Psalm 119:89)

READ

Amos 9:1-15

SEARCH THE SCRIPTURES

1. What kind of kingdom did Yahweh say his covenant people were to be in the following verses? What kind of kingdom does he call them in Amos 9:8? Why is this shocking?

"You will be for me a kingdom of priests and a holy nation." These are the words you are to speak to the Israelites. **(Exodus 19:6)**	*And you will be called priests of the Lord, you will be named ministers of our God.* **(Isaiah 61:6)**	*But you are a chosen people, a royal priesthood, a holy nation, God's special possession, that you may declare the praises of him who called you out of darkness into his wonderful light.* **(1 Peter 2:9)**	*To him who loves us and has freed us from our sins by his blood and made us a kingdom, priests to his God and Father.* **(Revelation 1:5-6 ESV)**

2. In the Israelite agricultural year, there was a dormant period. In the new system referenced in Amos 9:13, plowing for the grain crop would begin immediately after the harvest, suggesting great bounty and abundance.[1] And "as soon as someone sows the seed, the grapes grow so rapidly that the treader of grapes comes to pick the ripe grapes and gather them for the winepress."[2] What is characteristic of the harvest in the following passages?

Already the one who reaps is receiving wages and gathering fruit for eternal life, so that sower and reaper may rejoice together. **(John 4:36 ESV)**	*You have multiplied the nation; you have increased its joy; they rejoice before you as with joy at the harvest, as they are glad when they divide the spoil. For the yoke of his burden, and the staff for his shoulder, the rod of his oppressor, you have broken as on the day of Midian.* **(Isaiah 9:3-4 ESV)**	*"Behold, the days are coming," declares the LORD, "when the plowman shall overtake the reaper and the treader of grapes him who sows the seed; the mountains shall drip sweet wine, and all the hills shall flow with it."* **(Amos 9:13 ESV)**

3. Compare the imagery used in Joel with the imagery used in Amos. What imagery do the two prophecies share?

And in that day the mountains shall drip sweet wine, and the hills shall flow with milk, and all the streambeds of Judah shall flow with water; and a fountain shall come forth from the house of the LORD and water the Valley of Shittim. **(Joel 3:18 ESV)**	*"Behold, the days are coming," declares the LORD, "when the plowman shall overtake the reaper and the treader of grapes him who sows the seed; the mountains shall drip sweet wine, and all the hills shall flow with it."* **(Amos 9:13 ESV)**

4. In Luke 4:18, Jesus read the scroll from Isaiah 61, which spoke of restoration that included the poor and the oppressed. Consider how the prophets spoke of restoration. What is being restored in the following passages?

And your ancient ruins shall be rebuilt; you shall raise up the foundations of many generations; you shall be called the repairer of the breach, the restorer of streets to dwell in. **(Isaiah 58:12 ESV)**	*And I will vindicate the holiness of my great name, which has been profaned among the nations, and which you have profaned among them. And the nations will know that I am the LORD, declares the Lord GOD, when through you I vindicate my holiness before their eyes. I will take you from the nations and gather you from all the countries and bring you into your own land. I will sprinkle clean water on you, and you shall be clean from all your uncleannesses, and from all your idols I will cleanse you. And I will give you a new heart, and a new spirit I will put within you. And I will remove the heart of stone from your flesh and give you a heart of flesh.* **(Ezekiel 36:23-26 ESV)**	*They shall build up the ancient ruins; they shall raise up the former devastations; they shall repair the ruined cities, the devastations of many generations.* **(Isaiah 61:4 ESV)**	*I will restore the fortunes of my people Israel, and they shall rebuild the ruined cities and inhabit them; they shall plant vineyards and drink their wine.* **(Amos 9:14 ESV)**

REFLECT

Ask the Lord to give you a vision for restoration that moves you to participate in the work he's doing around you.

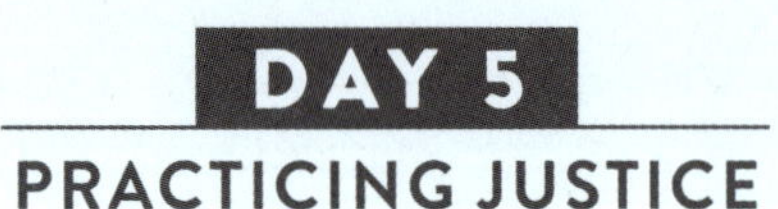

DAY 5

PRACTICING JUSTICE

Is not this the kind of fasting I have chosen: to loose the chains of injustice and untie the cords of the yoke, to set the oppressed free and break every yoke?

ISAIAH 58:6

PRAY

Father, please move me to compassion for the oppressed. Help me to be faithful to both pray and act by your Spirit, amen. (from Isaiah 58:6)

READ

Amos 9:1-15

RESPOND

1. Consider the definitions for *repair* and *raise up*. How might repairing and restoring look where you live? In your workplace?

2. If you could bring complete restoration to one area, what area would that be? How might you begin planting seeds for that restoration? What's one achievable action you can take in the next week?

3. Had you considered the work of rebuilding places and restoring people as a part of the gospel before this study? What, if anything, has challenged you to think differently about it?

4. Is there an area of injustice you feel particularly grieved by? With whom will you share this burden? What other actions might you take in response?

5. Read Isaiah 58:6-14. Based on this passage, how essential would you say that fasting and praying are for the work of restorative justice? How might this passage reorient your heart to this work? Consider reviewing it daily in the coming week.

BENEDICTION

"The days are coming," declares the LORD,

"when the reaper will be overtaken by the plowman
    and the planter by the one treading grapes.
New wine will drip from the mountains
    and flow from all the hills,
    and I will bring my people Israel back from exile.
They will rebuild the ruined cities and live in them.
    They will plant vineyards and drink their wine;
    they will make gardens and eat their fruit.
I will plant Israel in their own land,
    never again to be uprooted
    from the land I have given them,"
    says the LORD your God. (Amos 9:13-15)

Until the day when all things are made new, may you have a heart that is tender towards the disadvantaged and holy boldness to confront injustice. May you have uncommon wisdom in uncommon times. May the Spirit of the Lord strengthen, embolden, and replenish you as he uses your hands to rebuild and restore. Would radical neighbor love transform every place you stand in his name, amen.

NOTES

WEEK 1

[1]Abe Cho, *Idolatry & Pursuing Those on the Margins* (Redeemer City to City, 2022), video, www.globalfaithandwork.com/missionaldisciplevideos.

WEEK 2

[1]Willem A. VanGemeren, ed., *New International Dictionary of the Old Testament* (Zondervan, 1997), 3:557.

[2]Andrew E. Hill, *Amos*, The Gospel Coalition, accessed August 1, 2024, www.thegospel coalition.org/commentary/amos/.

[3]John H. Walton, Victor H. Matthews, and Mark W. Chavalas, *The IVP Bible Background Commentary: Old Testament* (InterVarsity Press, 2000), 767.

[4]Walton, Matthews, and Chavalas, *The IVP Bible Background Commentary.*

WEEK 3

[1]Tim Macke, *What's the Meaning of the Jewish Shema Prayer in the Bible?*, BibleProject, February 18, 2017, https://bibleproject.com/articles/what-is-the-shema/.

[2]Andrew E. Hill, *Amos*, The Gospel Coalition, accessed August 1, 2024, www.thegospel coalition.org/commentary/amos/.

[3]"The town of Bethel was located 12 miles or 19 kilometers north of Jerusalem on the Benjamin-Ephraim tribal border. The sites of Dan and Bethel were the locations where King Jeroboam established rival shrines housing golden calves so that the citizens of the northern kingdom would not be making pilgrimages to worship at the Jerusalem Temple (1 Kgs 12:25-30). Amos delivered his message in Bethel and condemned the idolatrous worship conducted there (Amos 4:4; 5:5-6; 7:10-13)." Hill, *Amos*, www .thegospelcoalition.org/commentary/amos/.

WEEK 4

[1]John H. Walton, Victor H. Matthews, and Mark W. Chavalas, *The IVP Bible Background Commentary: Old Testament* (InterVarsity Press, 2000), 769.

[2]Walton, Matthews, and Chavalas, *The IVP Bible Background Commentary*, 812.

WEEK 5

[1]Timothy Keller, *Generous Justice* (Dutton, 2010), 4.

[2]Keller, *Generous Justice.*

[3]Rabbi Yehuda (Ronnie) Warburg, "Mishnah Ketubot 4:4," www.sefaria.org/Mishnah_Ketubot.4.4?lang=bi.

[4]Soong-Chan Rah, *Prophetic Lament* (InterVarsity Press, 2015), Kindle.

[5]Andrew E. Hill, *Amos*, The Gospel Coalition, accessed July 27, 2024, www.thegospelcoalition.org/commentary/amos/#section-18.

[6]Duane A. Garrett, *Amos: A Handbook on the Hebrew Text* (Baylor University Press, 2008), 162-64.

[7]Timothy Keller, *Generous Justice* (Dutton, 2010), xiii.

[8]Rah, *Prophetic Lament*, Kindle, 7.

[9]Rah, *Prophetic Lament.*

[10]George Robertson, *Anatomy of the Soul* (New Growth Press, 2020), 3.

WEEK 6

[1]Strong's Lexicon, H2470, in the Blue Letter Bible, under "hala," accessed July 19, 2025, www.blueletterbible.org/lexicon/h2470/kjv/wlc/0-1/.

[2]Amos 6, ESV, accessed July 19, 2025, www.esv.org/Amos+6/.

[3]Duane A. Garrett, *Amos: A Handbook on the Hebrew Text* (Baylor University Press, 2008), 243-44.

[4]Garrett, *Amos*, 185.

WEEK 7

[1] Strong's Lexicon, H5162, in the Blue Letter Bible, under "naham," accessed July 20, 2025, www.blueletterbible.org/lexicon/h5162/kjv/wlc/0-1/.

[2]C. Hassell Bullock, *Prophetic Books: An Introduction to the Old Testament Prophetic Books* (Moody Press, 1986), 37.

WEEK 8

[1]Duane A. Garrett, *Amos: A Handbook on the Hebrew Text* (Baylor University Press, 2008), 287.

[2]John Oswalt, study note on Amos 9:13, *ESV Study Bible* (Crossway, 2008), 1,675.

RESOURCES

Arnade, Chris. *Dignity: Seeking Respect in Back Row America.* Sentinel, 2019.

Arnold, Bill T. and John H. Choi. *A Guide to Biblical Hebrew Syntax.* Cambridge University Press, 2003.

Barton, John. *Amos's Oracles Against the Nations.* Cambridge University Press, 1980.

Bonhoeffer, Dietrich. *Life Together: The Classic Exploration of Christian Community.* Harper & Row Publishers, Inc., 1954.

Brown, F., S. Driver, and C. Briggs. *The Brown-Driver-Briggs Hebrew and English Lexicon.* Hendrickson Publishers Marketing, LLC, 2014.

Bullock, C. Hassell. *An Introduction to the Old Testament Prophetic Books.* Moody Publishers, 2007.

Corbett, Steve and Brian Fikkert. *When Helping Hurts: How to Alleviate Poverty without Hurting the Poor . . . and Yourself.* Moody Publishers, 2012.

Garrett, Duane A. *Amos: A Handbook on the Hebrew Text.* Baylor University Press, 2008.

Heschel, Abraham J. *The Prophets.* HarperPerennial Modern Classics, 2001.

Keller, Timothy. *Generous Justice: How God's Grace Makes Us Just.* Riverhead Books, 2010.

Lockyer Sr., Herbert. *Nelson's Illustrated Bible Dictionary.* Thomas Nelson Publishers, 1986.

MacIntyre, Allister. *Whose Justice? Which Rationality?* University of Notre Dame Press, 1988.

The Navigators. *Minor Prophets 1: Hosea, Joel, Amos, Obadiah, Jonah & Micah.* NavPress, 2014.

Rah, Soong-Chan. *Prophetic Lament.* IVP Academic, 2015.

Redeemer City to City. *The Missional Disciple: Pursuing Mercy and Justice at Work*. Redeemer City to City, 2022.

Robertson, George. *Soul Anatomy: Finding Peace, Hope and Joy in the Psalms.* New Growth Press, 2020.

Stevenson, Bryan. *Just Mercy.* One World, 2014.

Taylor, Edward L. *The Words of Gardner Taylor Volume 5: Lectures, Essays, and Interviews.* Judson Press, 2001.

Thurman, Howard. *Jesus and the Disinherited.* Beacon Press, 1976.

Walton, John H., Victor H. Matthews, and Mark W. Chavalas. *The IVP Bible Background Commentary: Old Testament.* IVP, 2000.

FIGURE CREDITS

World Trade Center, Jacqueline Schmid via Pixabay

Map of Israel and neighbors, adapted from Bryan Windle, "Biblical Places on Modern Maps: Jordan," Bible Archaeology Report, April 7, 2018, https://biblearchaeologyreport.com/2018/04/07/biblical-places-on-modern-maps-jordan.

New York Skyline, Howard Huang via Photodisc

Supreme and Family Court, State of New York, Jim Henderson via Wikimedia Commons

Wall Street bull statue, Jeremy Huang via Unsplash

Map of Assyrian empire, adapted from David P. Barrett, "Israelites Are Exiled to Assyria," Bible Mapper Atlas, February 22, 2021, https://biblemapper.com/blog/index.php/2021/02/22/israelites-are-exiled-to-assyria.

San Juan Hill mural at Lincoln Center, courtesy of Vanessa K. Hawkins

The Bowery Mission, Ajay Suresh via Wikimedia Commons

Sunset over Manhattan, mshch via iStock / Getty Images Plus

Central Park Conservatory, Juliana Vilas Boas via E+ / Getty Images